Speak of me as I am

The Black presence in Southwark since 1600

by Stephen Bourne

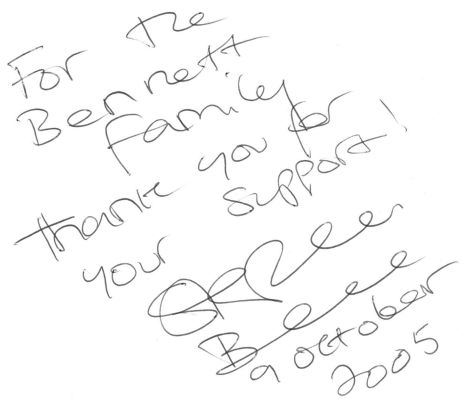

For the Bennett Family

Thank you for your support!

Stephen Bourne

October 2005

London Borough of Southwark

Southwark Local History Library
2005

Acknowledgements

Hakim Adi (Black and Asian Studies Association)
Mike Allport (Southwark Libraries)
John D. Beasley (Peckham Society)
Keith Bonnick (Cuming Museum)
Linda Bourne
Alex Brooke (Damilola Taylor sculpture)
Gill Davies (Strategic Director of Environment and Leisure, Southwark)
Stephen Douglass (Culture and Heritage Manager, Southwark)
Stephen Humphrey (Southwark Local History Library)
Richard Mangan (Mander and Mitchenson Theatre Collection)
S. I. Martin
Deborah Montgomerie
Richard Norman
Tim Otway
Marika Sherwood (Black and Asian Studies Association)
Robert Taylor
Keib Thomas
Val Wilmer

Arts Council England, London (Literature)
Black and Asian Studies Association
Cuming Museum (Walworth Road)
Southwark Bereavement Care
Southwark Local History Library (Borough High Street)
Theatre Museum (Covent Garden)

Contents

Acknowledgements ii

Dedication 1

Foreword by Sir Trevor Phillips 3

Spreading the Word 5

Chronology 12

1   Camberwell's First Black Citizen and Shakespeare's
Othello at the Globe 19

2   The Victorians: Ira Aldridge, Mary Seacole and
The Fisk Jubilee Singers 24

3   Edwardian Musical Theatre 36

4   Dr. Harold Moody 46

5   Paul Robeson and Elisabeth Welch 53

6   Sam King 62

7   When Denzel and *Desmond's* Came to Peckham 71

8   Marianne Jean-Baptiste 76

9   Rio Ferdinand 81

10   Southwark Connections 86

11   Southwark Culture and Heritage Services/Southwark Libraries 95

About the Author 99

Index 101

A Sculpture in Memory of the Life of Damilola Taylor
Created by Alex Brooke. Unveiled in June, 2002.
Photo: Robert Taylor

Stephen Bourne attended the Oliver Goldsmith Primary School on the corner of Peckham Road and Southampton Way from 1962 to 1969 and he dedicates this book to the memory of Damilola Taylor and pupils, past, present and future.

The following text has been contributed by Robert Taylor.

Damilola Taylor's death on the North Peckham Estate in South East London was one of 2000's biggest national news stories. At the time of his death he had been attending the Oliver Goldsmith Primary School for only three months and had yet to get the hang of things on the tough streets of Peckham. The senseless killing of a young Black child with so much ahead of him had a big impact in the area, particularly amongst parents and families in the local African and Caribbean communities. It was a powerful symbol, a point of focus for their anxieties about the many ways in which their children's prospects seem threatened or compromised by complex hostile forces beyond their control.

Mark Parsons, the Head Teacher at the school, wanted to create a permanent memorial to Damilola. He remarked, "Countless people in this country and around the world now know the name of Damilola Taylor. We can only hope that some good will come out of this terrible tragedy and that those responsible will acknowledge their guilt and find forgiveness. And we are left to celebrate how privileged we have all been to have known, albeit for such a short time, this beautiful, smiling child."

Together with the school governors, and in partnership with Damilola's family, Mark Parsons contacted the nearby Camberwell College of Arts and it was agreed that a number of students would be invited to submit designs. Three models were made and a single winner chosen. The sculpture by Alex Brooke – funded by the Community Chest and endorsed by Damilola's father – now stands just outside the school.

Alex, then a nineteen-year-old art student, wanted the sculpture to incorporate symbols of hope, regeneration and new life whilst also making reference to the theme of birds which often crops up in the folktales and tribal art of Nigeria, Damilola's birthplace. During her research she came across a picture of a Nigerian staff featuring a bird about to take off in flight. "It's like a phoenix taking off from the ashes," said Alex. "It's a symbol, not only to the memory of Damilola, but also for the whole of Peckham and its regeneration." The phoenix-like rising bird set in a circle does this with an elegant economy of gesture.

There is a dilemma for Mark Parsons and his team at Oliver Goldsmith Primary School. How to do enough in commemorating Damilola and what happened to him to satisfy the sensibilities and aspirations of his family and the local community, whilst not making so much of it that excessive fears, anxieties and concerns are generated amongst the children at the school.

One hopes in Alex's words that the memorial can be "a permanent focal point, a lasting dignified tribute in memory of Damilola and all that his life stood for".

Foreword
by Sir Trevor Phillips

People from African and Caribbean backgrounds have contributed to
Southwark's history – and that of many other British towns and cities –
for over five hundred years, and continue to do so. Though too often,
their pages have been omitted from the history books. From the
experiences of those ensnared by the slave trade; those who played vital
parts in the First and Second World Wars; those who've made their mark
in politics, right through to the entertainers and sportsmen who've
graced our stages and screens.

Traces of the many talents suppressed by the barbarism of slavery survive
through the records of the fortunate few Black people who were able to
fulfil some of their potential. Their names are still celebrated – like Mary
Seacole (see chapter 2) for her work in the Crimean War, or Olaudah
Equiano (c1745-1797) who published his best-selling autobiography, and
campaigned tirelessly against the slave trade.

Many of these remarkable people either have roots in Southwark, or links
to the borough through their work. Singers and music hall stars who
performed at the Camberwell Palace of Varieties (see chapter 3); Sam
King (see chapter 6), the first Black Mayor of Southwark in 1983; and
Rio Ferdinand (see chapter 9), the footballing superstar from Peckham –
have all enriched our local history.

Speak of Me As I Am teaches us a valuable lesson, allowing us to reinsert
a part of the past that is too often overlooked and ignored. Our history
is a rich tapestry. But somewhere along the line a few of the threads have
been pulled out. This book is about ensuring that some of those threads
are woven back into the tapestry, not left on the cutting room floor.

It gives us the opportunity to celebrate the contributions and achievements
made by Black settlers and their descendants which cut across the economy,
the world of politics, public service, law, medicine and the arts.

This adds immeasurably to the richness and creativity of modern Britain.

3

Trevor Phillips was appointed Chair of the Commission for Racial Equality on March 1, 2003. The Commission is based in Southwark (Borough High Street SE1). Trevor has campaigned on equality issues throughout his adult life. In 1998, his independent production company, Pepper Productions, produced the *Windrush* series for BBC television. This raised the profile of Britain's Black history.

Spreading the word

As a child in the 1960s I grew up in a racially-mixed, working-class community on a council estate in Peckham. From 1962 to 1969 I went to a culturally-diverse primary school on Peckham Road called Oliver Goldsmith.

In the 1960s Oliver Goldsmith included a new generation of children from African and Caribbean backgrounds: their parents had come to Britain as part of the large-scale post-Second World War migration of Commonwealth citizens. When I was a youngster, what British children of *all* cultural backgrounds were *not* made aware of – in schools, in history books, by the media, or by popular film and television – was that there had been a Black presence in Britain since at least the mid-sixteenth century. Black historical figures from the past had been made invisible, and there was a wall of silence around Britain's Black history. Regrettably, this is still the case.

Stephen Bourne and Eric Hinds, The Flower Festival, Oliver Goldsmith Primary School, July 10, 1963

However, I was lucky. I had an aunt who had been born Black and British long before the *Empire Windrush* (see chapter 6) docked at Tilbury in 1948 with the first wave of post-war Caribbean settlers. Unlike my contemporaries, my relationship to Aunt Esther, a Black Londoner born before the First World War, gave me, from an early age, an awareness of the pre-1948 Black presence in Britain. Consequently, I did not view the post-war settlers from the Caribbean as a 'threat', or agreed with those who, in the late 1960s, began suggesting that 'immigrants' be repatriated.

I was ten years old in 1968 when the Conservative MP Enoch Powell made his inflammatory 'River of Blood' speech on immigration from the Commonwealth. "In this country in 15 or 20 years' time the Black man will have the whip hand over the white man," Powell warned. "As I look ahead I am filled with foreboding. Like the Roman, I seem to see 'the River Tiber foaming with much blood.' " At the same time, in British homes up and down the country, his fictional disciple, Alf Garnett, shouted racist abuse in BBC television's *Till Death Us Do Part*. I was disgusted and it didn't surprise me that, as a teenager in the 1970s, I witnessed a rise in the popularity of the National Front. As long as I live I will never forget the horror of watching – from my bedroom window – members of the right-wing National Front march along Peckham Road with a police escort, which some of us interpreted as police protection. It didn't surprise me when, in 1981 and 1985, young – mostly Black – youths vented their anger and frustration on the streets of Brixton and Peckham. Clearly, growing up in a racially-mixed community, and having an aunt who was Black, gave me insights that most white children and teenagers in Britain did not get.

In 1974 I watched a fascinating television series on BBC-2 called *The Black Man in Britain 1550-1950* and this documented the history of Black people in Britain over 400 years. From this series I learned about Black historical figures and, hungry for more information, I was disappointed to find that, apart from the slave trade (always written from the white historian's perspective), there was no mention of Black people in our school history books. As a youngster I realised that my quest for knowledge would have to come from first-hand accounts, so I began to question Aunt

Stephen Bourne and Aunt Esther (1991)   *Photo: Val Wilmer*

Esther about her life. To my joy, I discovered that her stories were more interesting and relevant than the history I was being taught in school.

Aunt Esther – who worked as a seamstress from the age of fourteen until her retirement at the age of seventy-four – provided me with first-hand accounts of what life had been like for a working-class Black Londoner throughout the century. In the early 1900s, Joseph, her father, was an early pre-*Windrush* settler who had arrived in Fulham, west London from Guyana – then a British colony in South America. When Aunt Esther was a young child, he instilled in his daughter a sense of pride in her African heritage by teaching her about some well-known Black achievers, such as the Edwardian composer Samuel Coleridge-Taylor and the heavyweight world champion boxer Jack Johnson. In the 1930s Aunt Esther made dresses for the popular Black American entertainer Elisabeth Welch (see chapter 5) and befriended the Jamaican nationalist Marcus Garvey. She remembered the community spirit that existed during the Blitz, when she was 'adopted' by my great grandmother, and described the hardships faced by her cousin Leon and his family after they arrived here on 'a ship and a prayer' from Guyana in 1959. From my conversations with Aunt Esther

I learned about the importance of oral history testimony which has become a major feature of all my books, and in 1991 we published her life story.

The year 1974 was important to me for another reason. I left secondary modern school at the age of sixteen with no qualifications. At that time St. Michael and All Angels (now Archbishop Michael Ramsey Technology College) in Camberwell did not offer any useful qualifications and without them I was automatically disqualified from entering University and studying for a degree. So I went to work as a shop assistant in Rye Lane, Peckham. Needless to say, my passionate interest in Black British history took me on an educational journey I would not have missed for anything. I learned about a 'secret' history not found in conventional history books, or school texts. At first it was almost impossible to find information. In the 1970s my local libraries in Camberwell Church Street and Peckham Hill Street enabled me to access, through 'inter-library loans', some of the few books that did exist on the subject, including James Walvin's *Black and White: The Negro and English Society 1555-1945* (1973) and Folarin Shyllon's *Black People in Britain 1555-1833* (1977). These books opened up the subject in more ways than one, and from these authors I learned about many Black historical figures in Britain including Ira Aldridge (see chapter 2). The 1970s also saw the opening of the Peckham Bookplace at 13 Peckham High Street. This popular community bookshop aimed to serve the local multi-cultural community and stocked a wide range of books. I had never seen a Black literature section before. This was something new and exciting. At the Peckham Bookplace I discovered and purchased other pioneering works, including Edward Scobie's *Black Britannia – A History of Black People in Britain* (1972) and, in 1984, Peter Fryer's *Staying Power – The History of Black People in Britain* and the reissue of Mary Seacole's autobiography (see chapter 2).

The Bookplace also promoted community publishing, another innovative venture for Peckham, and for the next decade they published and distributed a number of books by local authors. I remember reading *Black Ink*, a collection of short stories, poems and plays by young people of African and Caribbean descent who went to school in the local area. Their writing was largely drawn from their personal experiences and from observations of the inner city environment in which they lived. Such books were primarily aimed at African and Caribbean teenagers in local secondary schools who were reluctant to read anything by the authors we found on our school curriculums, like Jane Austen, Charles Dickens and William Shakespeare. They also provided a valuable insight into the world of the African and Caribbean young, expressed in their own words and dialects. Sadly, by the early 1990s, the Peckham Bookplace had closed, and its innovative publishing ventures came to an end.

Meanwhile, in spite of being educationally disadvantaged at an early age, I graduated as a 'mature student' from the London College of Printing at the Elephant and Castle in 1988 with a Bachelor of Arts Degree in Film and Television. I also benefited from the existence of another local publisher, Hammersmith and Fulham's Ethnic Communities Oral History Project (ECOHP). This had been set up in the 1980s because members of local ethnic groups felt that their experiences were not being expressed in historical publications, exhibitions and educational resources. They also felt that false assumptions were being made about the countries where they or their parents were born. As a citizen of Fulham, Aunt Esther qualified as a subject for one of ECOHP's publications. With their enthusiastic support, *Aunt Esther's Story* was published in 1991 and for this we received the Raymond Williams Prize for Community Publishing. The book gave my aunt a sense of achievement and pride towards the end of her life. She died three years later in 1994 at the age of 81. Since that time I have continued to pursue a career as a historian of Black Britain, with two further publications for ECOHP.

It is intended that *Speak of Me As I Am – The Black Presence in Southwark Since 1600* will help broaden the range of books about Black British history and raise the profile of Black British historical figures who have been connected to the London Borough of Southwark. Among those included in the book are Ira Aldridge, Mary Seacole, Dr. Harold Moody, Paul Robeson, Elisabeth Welch, Sam King, Marianne Jean-Baptiste and Rio Ferdinand. Mainstream publishers rarely support such books. For example, non-fiction books in Black history sections of our bookshops and libraries are mainly imported from America and promote Black

Americans. Having worked as a part-time library assistant in Southwark since 2002, I am aware that local school children will occasionally enquire about Black historical figures such as Nelson Mandela, Martin Luther King and Rosa Parks, usually during Black History Month (October), but they do not ask about Black Britons from history.

When I gave a talk during Black History Month in 2004 for the Nunhead Library Teenage Reading Group, its members had never heard about the Peckham community leader Dr. Harold Moody (see chapter 4). They were not aware that Southwark Council had named the park near the library after him. Young people are interested in the subject of Black historical figures in Britain, but they are not told about them in school, or in history books, or in television programmes. Sam King (see chapter 6), a Jamaican who came to Britain on the *Empire Windrush* in 1948, and who became the first Black Mayor of Southwark, has expressed his concern that younger generations will not be informed about his generation's contribution to this country. He says, "A lot of people not given enough credit. We who came from the colonies survive alone till today. And in many areas we are contributing. And not enough credit is given to us by the youngsters, both Black and European. The neo-fascists are saying to us even now that we should go back. What do you think the authorities were saying in those days? But we survived. That's the only message I want. To let them know, we survived."

I had a similar reaction from the young Nigerian-born film director Newton I. Aduaka when I interviewed him about his Peckham-based film *Rage* in 2001: "There are Black kids that don't know anything about Black history. There are Black men and women who have gone through the school system here and know nothing about their history because they're not taught anything. If you didn't go out and search for it, you wouldn't know anything."

So I have been inspired to write *Speak of Me As I Am* as a result of my work with young people in the London Borough of Southwark, and hearing the concerns of Black citizens like Sam King who have made an important contribution to our way of life.

In addition to my work with Teenage Reading Groups at Nunhead and Peckham libraries, my work in this area has involved giving workshops at various youth centres (including the Sojourner Truth Centre in Peckham) and talks at events during Black History Month at venues such as Peckham Library and the Imperial War Museum, but there is still a wall of silence around the history of our nation's Black citizens. In my experience, in Britain, the media tends to ignore Black British history books, so those of us who write them have to find other ways to promote them, so that the public are made aware of their existence. For instance, *Aunt Esther's Story* sold out its first print run, but this was not because *The Guardian*, *The Independent* or *The Times Educational Supplement* reviewed it. They ignored it. So I took responsibility for much of the promotion myself by spreading the word at community level, handing out flyers, and leaving them on buses and tube trains, asking bookshop managers and libraries to stock it, and giving talks about it during Black History Month. It's exhausting, but this is what I do to promote my books about Black history in this country, and it is necessary if this wall of silence is to be broken down.

Note: In *Speak of Me As I Am* my use of the term Black means people of African descent, usually Black Americans (USA), or Black Africans and Caribbeans (Britain). I do not use the term 'immigrants'. I prefer to use 'settlers'. This book is not intended to be definitive; the reader will find many gaps. It reflects my interest in and knowledge of the performing arts, though I have dedicated chapters to some important community leaders, such as Dr. Harold Moody and Sam King.

Chronology

AD 208-211 Libya-born Roman Emperor, Septimius Severus, campaigned in northern England and Scotland, and restored Hadrian's Wall. He died in York in AD 211. The forces under his command had included Moors (north Africans).

AD 862 Vikings, returning from raids on Spain and North Africa, land Black slaves in Ireland.

10th Century evidence of Black settlers living in Norfolk.

In the Middle Ages, Africans were usually referred to as Blackamoors or Moors, the name given to the north African conquerors of Spain from 711 to 1492.

1500-1505 a small group of African servants are attached to the court of King James IV of Scotland.

1511 the painted roll of the Westminster Tournament, held to celebrate the birth of a son to Catherine of Aragon, includes the earliest pictorial record of a Black Briton. He is John Blanke, the trumpeter employed by Henry VII in 1507, and then by his successor, Henry VIII.

1555 a group of five Africans, from what is now Ghana, visit England to be trained as interpreters for English merchants.

During the reign (1558-1603) of Elizabeth I, England began to participate in the transatlantic slave trade.

1562-63 an unscrupulous adventurer, Sir John Hawkins, made the first English Atlantic slave voyage, acquiring at least 300 inhabitants of the Guinea coast.

From 1570 onwards some African slaves were brought to England to work as servants and entertainers, and there were African musicians and dancers at the court of Elizabeth I.

1595 William Shakespeare fell in love with a beautiful and famous African courtesan, Luce Morgan, also known as Lucy Negro or 'Black Luce', and some historians later identified her as his Dark Lady of the Sonnets.

1596 Elizabeth I issued a proclamation, ordering the expulsion of Black settlers from England.

1601 Elizabeth I issued a second Royal Proclamation, ordering the Lord Mayor of London to expel all 'negroes and blackamoors' from London.

1603 death of Elizabeth I.

1604 (November 1) William Shakespeare's tragedy *Othello* ("Speak of me as I am") first performed at the Whitehall Palace for King James. Other documented productions recorded during Shakespeare's lifetime include the **Globe Theatre** on **Bankside** in April 1610.

1607 (April 3) **John Primero**, "a negro", servant to Sir Thomas Hunt, was baptized at **St. Giles's Church** in Camberwell.

1615 (February 13) John Primero was buried at St. Giles's Church in Camberwell.

1698-1720 London became the leading slave port in Britain, followed by Bristol and Liverpool.

1731 The Lord Mayor of London banned Black people from becoming apprentices to any city trader. He did this to prevent any free Black citizen from making a living.

1733-34 painter and engraver William Hogarth featured a Black boy playing a trumpet in Southwark Fair. He used Black subjects in over two dozen of his works.

Mid-18th Century Black citizens could be found among the servant classes but there were a number of notable and accomplished Black figures of this period including the author Ignatius Sancho (1729-1780), whose portrait was painted by Thomas Gainsborough in 1768, and the abolitionist Olaudah Equiano (c1745-1797), who published his life story in 1789. This was widely used in the anti-slavery campaign.

1764 the Black population of London is estimated at 20,000 out of a total population of about 700,000.

1771-72 Somerset case: Lord Mansfield decided that a slave could not be removed from England against his or her will. This signalled the end of slavery in Britain.

1807 the abolition of the slave trade in Britain.

1815 many Black men fought in the Napoleonic wars, including the Battle of Waterloo. Some became Chelsea Pensioners.

1833 Shakespearean actor **Ira Aldridge** performed at the **Surrey Theatre** in **Blackfriars Road** in *Othello* and a selection of scenes from other plays.

1834 slavery was replaced by apprenticeship in British colonies.

1837 Queen Victoria's coronation.

1838 full freedom was granted in British colonies.

1848 (March 13) the Chartist movement for social and political reforms ended in a series of riots, one of which took place in **Camberwell** (Bowyer Lane, now Wyndham Road). This event included at least two Black demonstrators: David Anthony Duffy and Benjamin Prophett.

1848 **Ira Aldridge** returned to the **Surrey Theatre** in **Blackfriars Road** to play Othello.

1857 charity benefit held for the Jamaican nurse **Mary Seacole** at the **Royal Surrey Gardens** (near **Walworth Road**).

1860 violinist George Polgreen Bridgetower died at 8 Victory Cottages, Bedford Street (now Sandison Street) in Peckham.

1873 Morgan Smith played Richard III and Othello at the Surrey Theatre in Blackfriars Road.

1873 the Fisk Jubilee Singers performed at the Arthur Street Chapel in Camberwell Gate and Mr. Spurgeon's Metropolitan Tabernacle at the Elephant and Castle. They returned to the Tabernacle for a second engagement in 1874.

1894 a "Grand Production of Musical Tableaux Vivants" taken from Harriet Beecher Stowe's anti-slavery novel *Uncle Tom's Cabin* was presented at the South London Palace in London Road, near the Elephant and Castle. The programme promised "Beautiful Slave Pictures introducing Genuine Negroes recently arrived from the Southern section of the United States of America". These included Mr. Bill Edwards as Uncle Tom.

1900 a production of *Uncle Tom's Cabin* was staged at the Elephant and Castle Theatre. The cast included several Black actors including J. G. Johnston (as Uncle Tom) and Lizzie Allen (as Aunt Chloe) and, according to the programme, "Real Negroes" in the supporting cast.

1901 death of Queen Victoria.

1901-10 Edwardian music hall players including Belle Davis and Connie Smith appeared at the Camberwell Palace of Varieties.

1904 *In Dahomey* staged at the Crown Theatre, Peckham High Street.

1904 Harold Moody, age 22, came to England from Jamaica to study medicine at King's College. He qualified as a doctor in 1913.

1913 Dr. Harold Moody set up in practice at 111 King's Road (now King's Grove), Peckham.

1917 Charles Moody (see 1940) born at 111 **King's Road** to Dr. Harold Moody and his wife, Olive.

1921 Dr. Cecil Belfield Clarke opened his surgery in **Newington Causeway** near the Elephant and Castle. He practiced in the area for over forty years.

1922 Dr. Harold Moody moved to **164 Queen's Road SE15** where Peckham's only English Heritage Blue Plaque commemorates him.

1928 the most famous fight of the boxing champion **Len Johnson** took place at **The Ring** in **Blackfriars Road**. The Prince of Wales attended.

1931 the League of Coloured Peoples was founded in **Peckham** by **Dr. Harold Moody**, **Dr. Cecil Belfield Clarke**, and others. The LCP based itself in Moody's home, **164 Queen's Road SE15**, and was the most influential organisation that campaigned for the rights of African and Caribbean settlers in Britain.

1932 Jamaican poet **Una Marson** arrived in Peckham. The Moody family gave her a home. She later became the first Black woman programme maker and presenter on BBC radio.

1937 Paul Robeson made a personal appearance and gave a concert at the Elephant and Castle's **Trocadero Cinema** before a screening of his film *King Solomon's Mines.*

1940 Peckham-born **Captain Charles Moody**, son of **Dr. Harold Moody**, joined the Royal West Kent Regiment and became the first Black commissioned officer in the British army.

1944 Sam King, aged 18, left Jamaica and joined the Royal Air Force.

1946-50 Elisabeth Welch made several appearances at the **Camberwell Palace of Varieties** in the popular BBC radio series *Variety Bandbox.*

1947 Dr. Harold Moody died at the age of 64 and his funeral took place at the **Camberwell Green Congregational Church** in **Wren Road** (opposite Camberwell Green).

1948 (June 22) **Sam King**, aged 22, arrived at Tilbury with 492 other Jamaicans and Trinidadians on the *Empire Windrush*.

1950 Sam King and his family became the second to buy their own home in Southwark (**Sears Street** in **Camberwell**).

1954 (June 26) **Sam King** married student nurse Mavis Kirlew in **Emmanuel Church, Camberwell Road.**

1958 *West Indian Gazette* launched by Claudia Jones. **Sam King** employed as the circulation manager. He also becomes a member of the first Caribbean Carnival Committee.

1967 actress **Marianne Jean-Baptiste** born in St. Giles's Hospital, Camberwell.

1978 footballer **Rio Ferdinand** born in King's College Hospital, Lambeth.

1982 Sam King selected as Labour councillor for Bellenden ward.

1983 Sam King became the first Black Mayor of Southwark. Others have included **Cecile Lothian** (1993-94), **Aubyn Graham** (1995-96) and **Columba Blango** (2003-04).

1989 the first episode of the popular television series *Desmond's*, set in a **Peckham** barber shop, was screened on Channel 4 on January 5. It ended after its star, Norman Beaton, died on December 13, 1994, while visiting the land of his birth, Guyana.

1995 Dr. Harold Moody honoured with an English Heritage Blue Plaque at his former home in Peckham: 164 Queen's Road. It described him as a "campaigner for racial equality".

1996 Marianne Jean-Baptiste nominated for an American Oscar for the film *Secrets and Lies*.

1999 Marianne Jean-Baptiste gave an acclaimed portrayal of Doreen Lawrence in the television drama *The Murder of Stephen Lawrence*.

1999 Newton I. Aduaka's *Rage*, filmed on location in Peckham, was premiered in the London Film Festival.

2001 (October 31) Indian Bean Tree planted in Chumleigh Gardens (Burgess Park) in memory of **Dr. Harold Moody**.

2003 Rio Ferdinand honoured with a Southwark Council Blue Plaque. It overlooks the adventure playground in Peckham's Leyton Square.

Camberwell's first Black citizen and Shakespeare's *Othello* at the Globe

During the Christmas holidays of 2003 I browsed through my second-hand copy of William Harnett Blanch's *Ye Parish of Camberwell*, first published in 1875. This comprehensive history of Camberwell, described by Mary Boast in *The Story of Camberwell* (1996) as "a mine of information on Camberwell, Peckham and Dulwich", has always been one of my favourite books. Boast described Blanch as a local government officer, an Assistant Overseer of the Camberwell Vestry, who had access to all kinds of local archives. She also said that Blanch "spent two summer vacations at St. Giles's Church [Camberwell] studying the *Parish Registers* which were then stored in the vestry. The long extracts transcribed from such records make not only interesting reading, but are a very convenient source of material for the local historian."

If I have learned anything as a historian of Black Britain, it is not to be surprised to uncover new sources of information about the presence of people of African descent in our country. However, though I had read Blanch's fascinating book many times, there was a reference I had overlooked. With great surprise and interest I discovered on page 172

St. Giles's Church (2005)   *Photo: Tim Otway*

an entry for the baptism at St. Giles's Church on April 3, 1607 of "John Primero, a negro." The witnesses included Sir Thomas Hunt, Mr. Cox and Mrs. Mary Grymes. Another entry in Blanch's book revealed that John Primero died a few years later. The author added Primero's burial, registered at St. Giles's Church on February 13, 1615, "for Sir Thomas Hunt", who is described by Blanch as the "sheriff of Surrey and Sussex" (in 1610). Hunt died in Camberwell in 1625.

Who was John Primero? Blanch offers no explanation and, though his book has been available since 1875, no historian of Black Britain has mentioned Primero in their books. He has been completely overlooked. I have no idea where or when he was born. He could have been born in Africa or Camberwell. He could have been an adult or a child at the time of his baptism. In those days ages were not recorded in the baptism registers.

From 1570 onwards some African slaves were brought to Britain to work as household servants, and so it is likely that John Primero was a servant to Sir Thomas Hunt. At the time of John Primero's baptism, there may have been hundreds of Africans living in England, especially in London. Some records have survived of Africans living in towns such as Barnstaple in North Devon, and Plymouth.

In 1596 the importation of captive Africans taken from captured Spanish ships, and their replacement of English labourers, caused Queen Elizabeth I to issue an edict calling for their deportation. Primero may have already settled here by the time Elizabeth I made a second attempt to repatriate her Black citizens. In 1601 the Queen issued a Royal Proclamation stating that all 'Negars and Blackamoors' should be speedily expelled from England. She failed on both occasions. One thing is clear, if Primero had been here, he avoided repatriation. Primero may have been living in Camberwell when Elizabeth I died in 1603.

The Camberwell of 1607 was very different to the area we know today. When John Primero was associated with Camberwell it was a small village in the county of Surrey surrounded by – and famous for – its flowers and fruit trees. A Saxon church, mentioned in the Doomsday Book in 1087, existed on the site of St. Giles's Church and this was rebuilt in stone in

1152. Portions of this church existed to the time of its destruction by fire in 1841. John Primero was baptized and buried in this church. The present church on Camberwell Church Street was erected in 1844.

William Shakespeare wrote his famous play *Othello* a few years after Elizabeth I's Royal Proclamation. Shakespeare made the African, or Moorish general Othello, the hero of this play, and described him as brave and noble. In spite of their small numbers, Shakespeare had contact with at least one African in London. In the 1590s he befriended Luce Morgan – also known as Lucy Negro, or 'Black Luce' – a beautiful and famous African courtesan who ran a brothel in Clerkenwell, London. Apart from working as a servant, seamstress or prostitute, in those days there were few jobs available to Black women. Some authorities on Shakespeare believe that he fell in love with her, and at least one has identified her as Shakespeare's Dark Lady of the Sonnets.

John Primero may have been living in Camberwell on November 1, 1604 when Shakespeare staged *Othello* for the first time at Whitehall Palace for Elizabeth I's successor, King James. Primero was living in Camberwell when *Othello* was produced at the **Globe Theatre** on Southwark's Bankside in April 1610.

Othello was Shakespeare's second representation of an African character; the first was the villainous Aaron the Moor in *Titus Andronicus*. After *Othello*, two more Africans would appear in Shakespeare's plays: the Prince of Morocco in *The Merchant of Venice* and Queen Cleopatra in *Antony and Cleopatra*.

From October 7 to December 23, 2003, the Cuming Museum in Walworth Road SE17 presented *Lost and Found*, an exhibition exploring the early presence of Black African, Caribbean and Asian people in Southwark. Researchers from the London Metropolitan Archives viewed nearly 2000 Anglican Parish baptismal church records from 1536 to 1840, and provided an intriguing insight into the lives of these forgotten Black and Asian Londoners.

The database for the London Borough of Southwark records over 200 parish entries for Black Africans and Caribbeans who were baptized in the Borough during the period covered by the project. Most of the baptisms took place in the Southwark, Bermondsey and Rotherhithe areas, but there were a handful in St. Giles's, Camberwell. Historians of Black Britain have taught us that there were thousands of Black African and Caribbean people living in London during this period, but their presence has been largely forgotten over time.

The *Lost and Found* exhibition, curated by Keith Bonnick, focussed on the lives of several Black Africans who were baptised in Southwark between 1713 and 1800. These included the following: Elizabeth Williams, baptised on April 8, 1763 and described in the register as "a Negro servant to Capt. Millar". Captain John Millar lived in Rotherhithe's West Lane; Benjamin George Roberts, who was born a slave on a sugar plantation in the parish of Christ Church, Barbados in 1766. He was baptised on May 31, 1826 in the parish of St. Mary, Rotherhithe, at the age of 60 with his occupation recorded as a carpenter; and Juber Johnson, born in 1800, and baptised on January 22, 1816 in the parish of St. Mary Magdalen, Bermondsey. The parish register describes him as "a Black", records him as living at Printers Place and gives his occupation as seaman.

The earliest records in the database reveal ten baptisms in Southwark from 1609 to 1686. Though John Primero of Camberwell is missing from the database, it appears he was not the only Black citizen baptised in Southwark in the early 1600s. The earliest entry in the database is a baptism for a twelve-year-old "Blackmore" called Richard at Saint George the Martyr, Southwark, on February 19, 1609. The others are as follows:

Saint George the Martyr, Southwark
September 9, 1684 "Robert Adam a Blackamore about 18 years of age"
September 12, 1686 "William Incum a Blackmore about Nineteene or 20 years of age"

Saint Mary, Rotherhithe

January 7, 1682 "John Jarratson a blackamoore about 18 yeares old"
September 30, 1683 "Carles Thomas a blacamoore ffrom ye Ile of
St Thomas"

Saint Mary, Newington

March 17, 1682 "Grace Cornelius of ye Pish of new Christ Church a
Blackmore was Baptised"
September 15, 1683 "Elizabeth Hall a black-more"

Saint Thomas, Southwark

November 16, 1681 "Robert son of Quacco ffogg a Negro"

Saint Saviour, Southwark

October 11, 1668 "Ralph Truncket a Blackmoore aged 20 years willingly
bapt at Church"
August 8, 1686 "Mary Lucretia a Blackamore aged about 20 years"

It is generally believed that Africans and Caribbeans came to Britain after
the Second World War, and that their settlement in this country began
with the arrival of the *Empire Windrush* in 1948. Historians have
discovered that by 1764 there were 20,000 Black citizens in London when
the total population of the capital was only 676,250. The source for this
figure was found in an edition of *The Gentleman's Magazine* (vol. 34,
1764). It demonstrates that London's Black community has existed for
centuries, not decades.

The Victorians: Ira Aldridge, Mary Seacole and the Fisk Jubilee Singers

A number of important Black historical figures were associated with or connected to Southwark during the late eighteenth and nineteenth centuries. The violinist George Polgreen Bridgetower, the son of an adventurer, who described himself as a Barbadian, and a Polish countess, was amongst them. Beethoven described him as 'a very able virtuoso and an absolute master of his instrument.' Born in Poland in 1780, Bridgetower was a child prodigy who made his debut at the age of nine. In 1789, the young violinist performed at Windsor for King George III. A courtier said, "The young performer played to perfection, with a clear, good tone, spirit, pathos, and good taste." His first London appearance took place at the Drury Lane Theatre on February 19, 1790, when he played a concerto between the first and second parts of Handel's *Messiah*. He was accompanied by his father who, during the visit to London, dressed in extravagant Turkish robes, and was known as 'the Abyssinian Prince'. Bridgetower played in the Prince of Wales's band at the Royal Pavilion in Brighton for fourteen years. He died on February 29, 1860 at **8 Victory Cottages, Bedford Street** (now **Sandison Street**), **Peckham**, and was buried in Kensal Green Cemetery.

During Queen Victoria's reign (1837-1901) the main contact white Britons had with people of African descent was either in sport (primarily boxing) or in entertainment, but there were others. William Cuffay (1788-1870), born in Chatham, Kent to a freed slave, became one of the principal leaders of the London Chartist Movement, the forerunner to the Labour Party. Convinced that workers needed to be represented in parliament, Cuffay became involved in the first mass political movement of the British working-class. On March 13, 1848 two other Black chartists, David Anthony Duffy and Benjamin Prophett (known as 'Black Ben'), were among the leaders of a demonstration which took place in **Camberwell** (Bowyer Lane, now Wyndham Road). Both were arrested and transported to Australia. Cuffay, also transported to Australia, was later pardoned in 1856, but he decided not to return to England.

IRA ALDRIDGE

Ira Aldridge (1807-67) was one of the leading Shakespearean actors of the nineteenth century. In the Victorian era he became the first great Black American actor, although most of his appearances were in Britain or on the continent. His career spanned an awesome period of four decades, and he was known as 'The African Roscius' after Quintus Roscius Gallus, who was the most famous Roman actor of his day. Born in New York City, and intent on acting from an early age, Aldridge worked his passage to Liverpool as a ship's steward, and made his first known British performance on October 10, 1825 at London's Royal Coburg Theatre, later the Old Vic. He played Oroonoko in *The Revolt of Surinam, or A Slave's Revenge*. However, racist press hostility in the midst of the controversy over the abolition of slavery made it difficult for Aldridge to establish himself in London, though he worked a great deal in the provinces.

In April 1833 Aldridge made his West End debut as Othello at the Theatre Royal, Covent Garden, but the press did everything it could to destroy him. Despite a masterly performance, the theatre's leaseholder cut short Aldridge's engagement.

Afterwards, Aldridge accepted the first of two engagements at the **Surrey Theatre**. This was situated at the opening of **Blackfriars Road** at **St. George's Circus**. The Obelisk, a famous landmark, had been erected in the centre of St. George's Circus in 1771. The Surrey Theatre became the most famous and longest-surviving of the many 19th-century theatres and music halls of Southwark. It was finally demolished in 1934 to make way for an extension to the Royal Eye Hospital. More recently this has been demolished to make way for a student hostel.

Aldridge made his first appearance at the Surrey Theatre on April 22, 1833 in *Othello*. A Surrey Theatre playbill that has survived, dated May 20, 1833, advertises Aldridge in a selection of scenes from the following plays: *The Revenge* (as Zanga), *The Merchant of Venice* (as Shylock), *The Padlock* (as Mungo) and *The Castle Spectre* (as Hassan). Once again the press attempted to turn the public against him. The West End continued

Ira Aldridge as Aaron in Titus Andronicus (1852) (Mander and Mitchenson Theatre Collection)

to boycott him, but Aldridge did return to the Surrey Theatre for a second engagement in 1848. This time the press was kinder. For example, *The Times* (March 26, 1848) described his portrayal of Othello as "finely conceived and executed with great dramatic effect."

Frustrated by his failure to succeed in London, Aldridge successfully sought recognition on the continent. He also continued acting in the provinces and in Ireland. On his visits to Russia in 1858 and 1862 he introduced a less theatrical, more naturalistic acting style, and encouraged the production of Shakespeare's plays.

In 1855, after a long absence, Aldridge returned to London in triumph. He had now been honoured as the Chevalier Ira Aldridge, Knight of Saxony, and was allowed to perform at the Lyceum in 1858. He followed this with performances at St. Petersburg's Imperial Theatre, receiving great acclaim. One Russian critic, after seeing Aldridge's Othello, Lear, Shylock and Macbeth, said that those evenings 'were undoubtedly the best that I have ever spent in the theatre'. Another wrote, 'After Aldridge it is impossible to see Othello performed by a white actor.' At this time, an estimated three million Black Americans were slaves in the USA until the end of the Civil War in 1865. England's Anti-Slavery Society referred to Aldridge's majestic appearances on stage as significant contributions to the struggle for abolition. With his wealth he contributed to many fund-raising campaigns to end slavery in America. On November 3, 1863 he was granted British citizenship. Two years later he played Othello in an acclaimed production at London's Haymarket Theatre. He died, while on tour, in the Polish town of Lodz on August 7, 1867, aged sixty.

In *Ira Aldridge: The Negro Tragedian* (1958), Herbert Marshall and Mildred Stock describe him as: "The first to show that a black man could scale any heights in theatrical art reached by a white man – and recreate with equal artistry the greatest characters in world drama. He did this alone, without the aid of any social or political organizations...without any subsidies or scholarships, on his own two feet, with his own skill, versatility and talent. He did this in a white world, and showed that if a white can blacken his skin to represent Othello, then a black man can whiten his skin to represent Lear, Macbeth, or Shylock with equal artistry."

The name of Ira Aldridge has been inscribed with other Shakespearean actors at the Shakespeare Memorial Theatre in Stratford-upon-Avon. In 2004, Oku Ekpenyon, a member of the Black and Asian Studies

Association, successfully campaigned for Aldridge to be honoured at the Old Vic Theatre. The unveiling of a print of Aldridge as Aaron in Shakespeare's *Titus Andronicus* (donated by the National Portrait Gallery's collection) took place on September 24 that year.

MORGAN SMITH

Morgan Smith was a lesser-known Black Shakespearean actor of the Victorian era. Born in 1833 in Philadelphia, he found American theatres unwilling to employ him. Realising that there was no future for him as an actor in America, he moved to England in 1866. Within days of arriving he leased a theatre in Gravesend, Kent and, despite having never acted before, he appeared as Othello, Richard III, Macbeth, Hamlet, and Shylock over the next month. The season, which ran from May 19 to June 16, was not a financial success, but it earned Smith favourable reviews and within four months of arriving in the country, he made his London debut on August 25 at the Olympic Theatre playing Othello. A successful career

Surrey Theatre, St. George's Circus, 1812 (Southwark Local History Library)

followed during which he commissioned various plays involving Black characters, but he also continued to perform Shakespearean roles, such as Richard III, which were not written for a Black actor. In May 1873 Smith was engaged at the **Surrey Theatre** playing, amongst others, Richard III and Othello. The 1881 Census confirms that Smith, age 48, an actor, was lodging in York with his wife, Hannah, and their son, Edgar, who had been born in Hammersmith, London in 1867. Smith died in Sheffield in 1882.

When Errol Hill assessed Smith for his book *Shakespeare in Sable – A History of Black Shakesperean Actors* (1984), he said, "As an interpreter of Shakespeare, Morgan Smith cannot be ranked with Ira Aldridge. He lacked that spark of greatness that is reserved for the privileged few whom the gods love. He did not have Aldridge's range and emotional power...Smith was more the master of pathos than of righteous anger. He was, nonetheless, a superior performer, a talented and painstaking actor of intelligence...he was unquestionably a worthy successor to the great black tragedian [Aldridge]."

MARY SEACOLE

Born in 1805 in Kingston, Jamaica, Mary Seacole, the daughter of a Scottish army officer and a Jamaican boarding-house owner, learned herbal medicine and folk remedies from her mother. She became an experienced 'doctress' who often treated British soldiers stationed in Jamaica. On hearing about the terrible conditions in the Crimean War, Seacole, convinced that her knowledge of tropical medicine would be of service, travelled to London in October 1854 and applied for a position as a nurse. Despite her references from army doctors, Seacole was turned down. Undeterred, Seacole borrowed sufficient money to make the 4,000-mile journey to the battlefields. After arriving at Balaklava in February 1855, Seacole nursed sick and wounded British troops, and risked her own life by carrying them off the battlefields. She was known as "Mother" or "Aunty" Seacole. A lieutenant in the 63rd (West Suffolk) regiment wrote in his memoirs: "She was a wonderful woman...All the men swore by her, and in case of any malady would seek her advice and use her herbal medicines, in preference to reporting themselves to their

Mary Seacole (National Portrait Gallery, London)

own doctors. That she did effect some cures is beyond doubt, and her never failing presence among the wounded after a battle and assisting them made her beloved by the rank and file of the whole army."

Noticed in the dispatches of William Howard Russell, the war correspondent for *The Times*, for her courage under fire and comforting presence to the wounded, he wrote, 'She is always in attendance near the battle-field to aid the wounded, and has earned many a poor fellow's blessings'. Seacole was the first woman to enter Sevastopol when it fell after a long siege. When the peace was suddenly concluded she returned to Britain in July 1856. Seacole was decorated for her work, and gained the admiration and affection of Queen Victoria. At a 'Dinner for the Guards' held at the **Royal Surrey Gardens** in August, 1856, she was a guest of honour, but, in spite of her fame, she was almost destitute. However, Lord Rokeby, who had commanded a division in the Crimea, and others, organized for her benefit a gigantic four-day musical festival at the **Royal Surrey Gardens**, in Penton Place in Walworth. Almost 1,000 performers, including nine military bands and an orchestra, took part. At the end of both parts of the programme her name was, said a reporter in *The Times* (July 28, 1857), 'shouted by a thousand voices' and 'the genial old lady rose from her place and smiled benignantly on the assembled multitude, amid a tremendous and continued cheering'. After returning home to Jamaica for several years (1859-65), Seacole settled in London where she died in 1881.

In 1857 William Howard Russell wrote the introduction to her best-selling autobiography. Unlike her contemporary Florence Nightingale, Seacole's life was not remembered in our history books. For almost a century after her death, she remained in obscurity. Seacole was rediscovered in the 1970s and 1980s, and three individuals stand out for their roles in promoting a new awareness of her historical importance: Connie Mark, founder of the Mary Seacole Memorial Association, and Ziggi Alexander and Audrey Dewjee, editors of the first reprint of her autobiography in 1984. In 1973, Seacole's grave was restored after being rediscovered by Jamaican nurses in the Kensal Green Roman Catholic cemetery, west London. In 2004 she was voted the Greatest Black Briton in an online poll.

FISK JUBILEE SINGERS
In 1873, eight years after the end of slavery in America, a new kind of music was heard in London, which had critics and royalty alike singing its praises. The Fisk Jubilee Singers toured Britain for the first time that year, having already introduced American audiences to Negro Spirituals, sombre, majestic songs about slavery. Said Peter Fryer in *Staying Power – The History of Black People in Britain* (1984): "In a world without gramophone, radio, and television, travellers alone had access to such music. And both the songs and the way they were sung had a powerful impact on everyone in Britain who heard them." The choir was formed in Tennessee, where many newly-liberated slaves were educated. There were eleven in number – seven women and four men, and eight of the eleven were former slaves. Their aim was to raise funds for the newly-established Fisk University, for Black students, in Nashville. In 1873 they made their first fund-raising trip abroad, and it was to Britain they came.

The first wave of popularity took them to London where the choir gave a private performance to members of Parliament, church leaders and journalists. Organised by the Earl of Shaftesbury, President of the Freedmen's Missions Aid Society, the concert took place at Willis's Rooms on May 6. The concert was also attended by the Duke and Duchess of Argyll who arranged for the singers to perform at Argyll Lodge the next

The Fisk Jubilee Singers (Stephen Bourne)

day. The visit was destined to be a more notable event than they could ever have imagined, for Queen Victoria had been asked to attend. The event was described in *The Story of the Jubilee Singers* (1876),

> They had been told, again and again, that if they could but sing before the Queen their success would be assured...Soon after her Majesty's arrival, the Duke informed them that she would be pleased to see them in an adjoining room. At his request they sang, first, "Steal Away to Jesus", then chanted The Lord's Prayer, and sang "Go Down, Moses." The Queen listened with manifest pleasure, and, as they withdrew, communicated through the Duke her thanks for the gratification they had given her. There was no stage parade or theatric pomp in the scene; but the spectacle of England's Queen coming from her palace to listen to the songs which these humble students learned in their slave cabins.

Maggie Porter, a member of the choir who had been born into slavery in 1853, later recalled, "The Queen wore no crown, no robes of state. But it was the Queen in flesh and blood. I saw her, I heard her deep, low voice saying, 'Tell them we are delighted with their songs'. I wondered why the Queen did not speak these words to us. We were within hearing."

"They are real Negroes," wrote Queen Victoria in her journal that night, "come from America & have been slaves. They sing extremely well together." The Queen's pleasure opened doors for the choir. Prime Minister Gladstone, The Prince of Wales, dukes, duchesses and earls, were transfixed by their songs. And the singers were quickly embraced by evangelicals crusading to save British souls.

Charles Haddon Spurgeon (1834-1892), one of the greatest Victorian Baptist preachers, expounded a simple fundamentalist faith in a riveting manner. He was the founder of the great **Metropolitan Tabernacle**, built for him in 1859-61 at the **Elephant and Castle**. It was the largest Protestant church in London, seating over six thousand. It was filled to capacity whenever Spurgeon preached. Spurgeon was one of the ministers who recognized that an upper-class church had little to offer "the common people."

Always sympathizing with the oppressed, it did not surprise anyone that the Fisk Jubilee Singers received an invitation from Spurgeon and the deacons to give one of their concerts at the **Metropolitan Tabernacle**. A vast mass of people crowded into every inch of space in the building to hear them. Indeed, hundreds had to be turned away. The collection that followed cleared about £220, a huge sum in those days, for their University by singing in the Tabernacle alone.

Before the Fisk Jubilee Singers made their first appearance at the Tabernacle, they made an appearance in Southwark that has not been recorded. Searching through *The South London Press* at Southwark's Local History Library, I uncovered the following announcement in the June 28, 1873 edition:

The Jubilee Singers (from Fisk University, Nashville,
Tennessee, U.S.A.) will appear at Arthur Street Chapel,
Camberwell Gate, on Friday, July 4, at 8 o'clock precisely.
Tickets may be obtained of Mrs. Wilmot, 298 Walworth
Road, near Carter Street.

The Sunday before they made their historic appearance at the
Tabernacle, they attended a service there, and at the close greeted
Mr. Spurgeon. On July 26, 1873, *The South London Press* announced their
historic appearance at the **Metropolitan Tabernacle**:

On Wednesday, July 30, 1873, the Jubilee Singers of Fisk
University, Nashville, U.S.A. will give a service of song in
the above place, being their last appearance, previous to
their leaving for Scotland. C. H. Spurgeon will preside.
Doors open at 7. Commence at half-past.

The following is an extract from a lengthy review of the concert that
appeared in *The South London Press* on August 2, 1873:

the Tabernacle was crowded, and a hearty burst of applause
greeted both singers and Mr. Spurgeon as they came on to
the platform. In the course of a few introductory remarks,
Mr. Spurgeon said, 'We are gathered in a remarkable
manner to celebrate the death of slavery – some time after
its death, perhaps, in America, but not so long when we
remember the trafficking in human flesh in other parts of
the world...Our friends will sing to you some of the songs
such as they used to sing in the old slave time...They seem
to have something about them which I have never heard
before in anything ever given in the way of a performance.
Our friends seem to sing from their hearts. They seem to
preach in their singing, and this gives a force to the music
such as no other thing could. They have touched my
heart...There is a real mystery and a deep theology in this
singing that we can hardly understand. We have not been

placed under the same circumstances. Very few of us have had our backs tingling under the lash, and have never had to work in a cotton plantation; we have never known what it is to be without the things we enjoy now.' (Cheers). The performers then sang the first on the programme. "Steal Away to Jesus"…The song terminated with the chanting of The Lord's Prayer. The next song was entitled "Go Down, Moses" and the applause which followed was almost deafening. Among the other songs which were given were "Many Thousands Gone", "John Brown's Body", "Mary and Martha", "Roll, Jordan, Roll", "Turn Back Pharoah's Army", "Swing Low, Sweet Chariot" and many others.

The Metropolitan Tabernacle (2005)   *Photo: Tim Otway*

Edwardian musical theatre

IN DAHOMEY IN PECKHAM

In Dahomey was the first full-length musical written, performed and staged by Black artistes. Among the stars were the comedy team Bert Williams (1874-1922) and George Walker (1873-1911). They were already big names in American vaudeville when they came to London. The *In Dahomey* company came to the Shaftesbury Theatre in London's West End from New York in 1903 and became the 'in' thing to see. Music historian Jeffrey Green says: "It was word of mouth recommendation. Curiosity, because it was an all-Black show, leading to people saying 'You must go and see Williams and Walker, you must go and see *In Dahomey*, it's so funny, so lively.' That led to the contract being extended. It played from May 1903 into Christmas of 1903 when the Shaftesbury Theatre was closed for redecoration. Then it toured all over England into Scotland. So it was in Britain for well over a year."

In Dahomey was such a hit with the British public that the cast were invited to perform at Buckingham Palace on June 23, 1903. The Royal family were celebrating the ninth birthday of Prince Edward (later the Duke of Windsor). He and his brother, who was the present Queen Elizabeth's father, George VI, were there for the party with 150 other children and the *In Dahomey* cast entertained them. King Edward VII himself was also present, and he sent one of his noblemen to ask if the cakewalk being performed was the genuine article. So the Black American cast of *In Dahomey*, within five weeks of their arrival in London, were playing before the King Emperor. This was, of course, reported by the Black and white American press and this gave the show an enormous amount of prestige.

On April 2, 1904 one of our local newspapers, the *South London Observer and Camberwell and Peckham Times*, made the following announcement for the **Crown Theatre** in **Peckham High Street**:

> Next week Messrs. Williams and Walker and the whole of the original company from the Shaftesbury Theatre will appear here in the negro opera, "In Dahomey," which should prove a big attraction for the holidays. With

Bert Williams and George Walker (Stephen Bourne)

characteristic modesty Messrs. Hurting and Seaman
announce that "the company of first-class artistes that has
been selected for this production is from the very best in
the theatrical firmament, and can sing, dance, and act."
Peckham playgoers, please note!

In Dahomey played at the **Crown Theatre** in **Peckham High Street** for one
week commencing April 4, 1904. The Theatre had opened in 1898, five
years after the Police Station was built a few yards away. In 1912 the
theatre was called the Peckham Hippodrome Picture Palace. After being
demolished, it was replaced by the Gaumont Palace Cinema in 1932. In
the 1970s it was converted into a bingo hall, but the building was recently
torn down to make way for Gaumont House, an apartment block.

Bert Williams helped change the face of American entertainment.
Vaudeville had been seen as a white's only tradition before he burst onto
the scene. It might seem crazy now, but when Bert Williams sang he was
forced to do what white performers did and put on black face make-up.
But by doing this he paved the way for countless Black artistes to follow
in vaudeville and musical theatre.

The Crown Theatre, Peckham. 1898 (Southwark Local History Library)

Belle Davis (Rainer E. Lotz)

Bert was famous for playing an amiable character who was down on his luck, and he wore a shabby dress suit and shoes three sizes too big. He had a theme song called 'Nobody' that audiences demanded to hear whenever he appeared. In fact, it was linked to his name as closely as 'Old Man River' was later associated with Paul Robeson.

BELLE DAVIS

Belle Davis was one of the most popular stars of Edwardian music halls. Born in New Orleans about 1874, of European and African ancestry, the tall, beautifully dressed soprano spent most of her adult life in Britain. She differed from most Black singers of her generation by performing songs that were not from the minstrel show or spiritual traditions, but were graceful melodies. She also presented herself on stage as a sophisticated, elegant woman of the world, not a bandanna-wearing 'Aunt Jemima'.

Belle first toured Britain in a show called *Oriental America* in 1897-98. Returning here in 1901, Belle became one of the first Black women to have her voice recorded. In London in 1902 she recorded one of the most popular music hall songs of the day, 'The Honey-Suckle and the

Camberwell Palace of Varieties (Southwark Local History Library)

Bee'. In spite of her success and popularity – she toured Britain extensively from 1901 to 1918 – there has been very little acknowledgement of her achievements.

Following a busy tour that took her to music halls all over London, including Brixton, Walham Green and Clapham, Belle made the first of several appearances at the **Camberwell Palace of Varieties** on November 24, 1902. Mary Boast describes the **Palace** in *The Story of Camberwell* (1996) as one of the grand, purpose-built theatres that were built in many London suburbs in the 1890s. "Camberwell excelled in having two of these," she says, "almost facing each other across Denmark Hill. On the east side was the Oriental Palace of Varieties, built in 1896. In 1899 it was rebuilt as the Camberwell Palace, with seating for over 2,000 people. Famous old timers who appeared here included Marie Lloyd, Harry Lauder, Nellie Wallace and Harry Tate. The Camberwell Palace finally closed in 1956. Only a small street named after Orpheus, the musician of ancient Greek legend, marks the site of Camberwell's own music hall."

Return engagements for Belle to the **Camberwell Palace** followed in 1903 and 1906. By the outbreak of World War One in 1914, Belle had been seen in music halls all over the country. Still headlining in **Southwark** during the First World War, an advertisement in the *South London Press* (May 12, 1916) announced that 'Belle Davis and her Crackerjacks' would be appearing 'Monday Next, and during the week, Twice Nightly' at the **South London Palace** with a supporting cast that included 'Mr Walton with his musical and trick poodle dogs'.

In the 1920s, Belle worked mostly in Paris. From 1925 to 1929 she directed the dancing in several revues at the Casino de Paris, but she disappears after 1929. It is likely she died in France in the 1930s. In 1997 the German historian of jazz, Rainer E. Lotz, included a survey of Belle's career in his book *Black People: Entertainers of African Descent in Europe and Germany* and illustrated this with several rare photos of the beautiful star.

Connie Smith (Stephen Bourne)

CONNIE SMITH
For many years
Connie Smith was
Britain's oldest and
most respected Black
actress. She also
influenced young
Black actors and
actresses in this
country, including
Pauline Henriques,
who remembered:
"On stage she had
a presence, even
though she was very
small and very quiet.
She had discipline
and a subtle way of
playing. I would say
Connie was the first
Black professional in
the theatre that I ever
met. She would be on time for rehearsals and she never missed a cue.
However tiny the part was, she studied it meticulously. Connie was always
encouraging to younger actors, especially those of us who were Black.
I recognised that she had something very few Black actors have had –
enormous experience. After all, her theatre career spanned from the
1890s to the 1960s."

Born Cornelia Johnson in Brooklyn, New York in 1875, in the mid-
1890s, young Connie left New York to tour Germany and Denmark in a
stage production of *The South Before the War*. It was during that tour that
she met and fell in love with 'Gus' Smith, a pianist and variety artist from
Philadelphia. In 1895, they travelled to Britain, where they were booked
to appear at the Alhambra Theatre in Hull. Billing themselves as Smith
and Johnson, they found plenty of work in music halls and were among

the first Black artists to perform the cake-walk, a popular dance craze of the period, in Britain. Their piano duets – with Augustus in white gloves on bass and Connie playing the melody – claimed encore after encore. In 1902 a critic described their appearance at Sheffield's Grand Theatre of Varieties as "duettists and cake-walkers who give their amusing turn to appreciative applause".

A painstaking search for a copy of their marriage certificate has resulted in an entry being found in the records for 1902. Levi Augustus Smith married Cornelia Estelle Johnson on May 1 that year in a Catholic ceremony at St. Francis Xavier's Church in Everton, near Liverpool.

In Edwardian Britain, Black entertainers were still looked upon as novelties – and in some parts of the country, many people had never seen a Black person. So when Smith and Johnson visited places like Southwark to perform in theatres such as the **Camberwell Palace of Varieties**, there was much pointing and staring. Yet Connie later recalled: "We never had any sort of insult or suffered any indignity from the British." She also remembered how evenings spent at music halls – before radio and television existed – provided magic for the British public.

In 1914, at the outbreak of the First World War, as American citizens, Connie and her husband were offered their fares home, but they declined. In fact, Britain became their adopted home, and to the day she died, Connie never saw America again.

After Gus died on January 6, 1927, Connie was heartbroken but she kept working. In 1927, she appeared as Aunt Chloe in a special prologue staged at the London Pavilion in Piccadilly Circus before the screening of the silent film *Uncle Tom's Cabin*. The following year, she returned to the London Pavilion to take part in a charity concert described as "the greatest all-star coloured show ever staged". It was organised to raise money for the victims of flooding caused by the swollen River Thames.

Lyricist Oscar Hammerstein II and composer Jerome Kern were in the audience, taking notes for the casting of their forthcoming Drury Lane

St. George's Cathedral (2005)   *Photo: Tim Otway*

production of *Show Boat*. Consequently Connie was invited to understudy
Alberta Hunter as Queenie, and sing with the Mississippi Chorus,
backing Paul Robeson (see chapter 5) when he sang his famous 'theme
song', "Old Man River".

In London, Connie became well known among agents, producers and playwrights, and made a successful transition from music hall player to character actress. Whenever there was a part for an older Black woman, she was considered. Her earliest dramatic roles included Addie in the West End stage version of Lillian Hellman's *The Little Foxes* (1942) and the mother of Elisabeth Welch (see chapter 5) in the BBC radio play *Broadway Slave* (1944). Just after the war, she became one of the first Black actresses to appear on British television when she portrayed Mrs. Harris in Eugene O'Neill's *All God's Chillun' Got Wings*, produced by the BBC in 1946.

After the war, Connie found herself in more demand than ever. For example, in 1956, at the age of eighty, she became a member of the distinguished English Stage Company at London's Royal Court. Her roles included the sorceress Tituba in Arthur Miller's *The Crucible* and Granny in *Flesh to a Tiger*, written by the Jamaican dramatist Barry Reckord.

In 1961 she made her last stage appearance in a German production of Eugene O'Neill's *The Emperor Jones*, learning to cope with a foreign language at the age of eighty-six. Ill health forced Connie into retirement and eventually she had to leave her Brook Drive home, on the border of Lambeth and Southwark, when she was admitted to St. Peter's House, a Catholic nursing home in Meadow Road, Lambeth.

Connie died on May 11, 1970 at the age of ninety-five. On May 18, a mass was read for her at **St. George's Roman Catholic Cathedral** in Lambeth Road, Southwark, just prior to her funeral service. She was buried in the famous variety artists' section of Streatham Park Cemetery in an unmarked grave, a fitting resting place according to Pauline Henriques: "It doesn't surprise me that Connie is buried in an unmarked grave, because she underplayed everything. She would be perfectly happy with that."

Dr. Harold Moody

The following memories of Dr. Harold Moody have been provided by one of his former patients, Ron Woollacott, who pays tribute to the doctor in his unpublished autobiography, *Growing Up in Peckham 1942-1960*. Dr. Moody practised in Peckham from before the First World War, to the 1940s. This would have been in the days before Britain had a National Health Service, and working-class families faced hardship when they tried to find money to pay doctors for medical treatment. Dr. Moody often treated the children of working-class families for no charge. Ron says,

> My mother brought me to live in Peckham in the summer of 1942. I was a sickly child and suffered from what was generally known then as a weak chest but was later diagnosed as bronchial asthma. We lived in Geldart Road but I can't remember how many times I visited Dr. Moody at his Queen's Road surgery. It was quite a few, and I have a clear mental picture of the doctor as there were few Black people in Peckham at the time. I remember him as a kind and gentle man, not at all stern or grumpy as some doctors might have appeared to children. My late mother said Dr. Moody was well liked and well known for treating children sympathetically. I seem to recall he was an elegant, bespectacled gentleman, always smartly dressed in a dark suit and a neat collar and tie, with a stethoscope around his neck. I recall he always warmed his stethoscope by a radiant gas fire before placing it on my chest. I had never seen a gas fire before. It is worth noting that Dr. Moody was our doctor before the dawn of the welfare state and free medical care in 1948.

However, Dr. Moody was more than just a popular family GP. He was an ambassador for Britain's Black community, and an important figurehead who campaigned to improve the situation for African and Caribbean settlers in Britain.

Dr. Harold Moody was born in Kingston, Jamaica in 1882, the eldest son of a middle-class family. He came to England at the age of twenty-two in

Dr. Harold Moody (Stephen Bourne)

1904 to study medicine at King's College Hospital, then situated in Lincoln's Inn Fields and now at Denmark Hill, but the 'Mother Country', as it was then known, was totally ignorant of life in the colonies. The young Moody was completely unprepared for Edwardian London, and found it hard to find lodgings. He was often confronted by English people raised on images of slavery and savagery. They were shocked to meet an educated, well-spoken Black man who appeared to be more English than themselves.

Having won several academic awards, Moody qualified as a doctor in 1912, but, though he was the best applicant, he was denied a position at King's College Hospital because of open racism. He also applied for an appointment as one of the medical officers of the Camberwell Board of Guardians. A doctor who was a member of this Board stated publicly that Dr. Moody had the best qualifications of all the applicants, but that the "poor people would not have a nigger to attend them." Dr. Moody was not given the appointment. Of this incident he wrote, "I retreated gracefully and applied myself to the building up of my private practice."

Forced into self-employment, Dr. Moody started his own practice at 111 King's Road (now King's Grove), Peckham in 1913. That same year he married Olive Tranter, a warm, affectionate English nurse, and they had six children: Christine (1914), Harold (1915), Charles (1917), Joan (1918), Ronald (1920) and Garth (1925), who became a religious minister.

Dr. Moody's experiences of hardship and racist attitudes led him to become one of the founders of the League of Coloured Peoples (LCP) in 1931. Its first meeting took place at the Central YMCA, Tottenham Court Road, on March 13, 1931. Dr. Moody was its first president, and the LCP based itself at his second Peckham home. In 1922 Dr. Moody had moved his family to **164 Queen's Road**, a spacious, rambling Victorian house. This is now marked with an English Heritage Blue Plaque in Moody's honour.

One of the League's founder members was another eminent doctor, Cecil Belfield Clarke. Born in Barbados in 1894, he came to England with a scholarship to study medicine in 1914. After qualifying as a doctor, he practised in Southwark for nearly fifty years at his surgery, 112 **Newington Causeway**, near the **Elephant and Castle**. In addition to his support for the LCP, Dr. Belfield Clarke was elected the first Chairman of the House Committee of Aggrey House, a hostel for Black students in Britain. He also supported the work of the West African Students Union. His house at Barnet was described as 'a great Commonwealth Centre', and he had a special interest in cementing friendships and understanding between people from Africa and the Caribbean. Despite a busy professional life, coupled with his involvement in Commonwealth affairs, Dr. Belfield Clarke followed very keenly local affairs both in Southwark and Barnet. He gave up his practice in Newington Causeway in 1965, and died on November 28, 1970.

Another important figure who worked with the LCP was the Jamaican poet, Una Marson (1905-1965). As a young woman in Jamaica, Una set up the Jamaican Save the Children Fund, and pleaded the cause of Rastafarian children. Coming to England in 1932, she was helped by Dr. Moody and his family who gave her a home at 164 Queen's Road, where she worked as secretary to the LCP. Before long she became well known in London as a feminist activist who campaigned on Black women's issues, such as discrimination in the nursing profession. She also lived for a while at **Brunswick Square** in **Camberwell**, but often journeyed abroad. Una Marson became the first Black woman programme maker at the BBC where she worked from 1939 to 1946. As the presenter of BBC radio's *Calling the West Indies*, she helped many Caribbean service men and women stay in touch with their families during the war. Widely respected, she counted such literary figures as George Orwell and T. S. Eliot among her BBC colleagues.

Dr. Moody saw the LCP primarily as serving a Christian purpose, not a political one. For two decades the LCP was the most influential organisation campaigning for the civil rights of African and Caribbean people in Britain. The visitor's book on display in their home read like a who's who of Black historical figures. The visitors included Paul Robeson (see chapter 5), the Trinidadian historian and novelist C. L. R. James, Kwame Nkrumah, who became President of Ghana, and Jomo Kenyatta, who became the founding President of the Republic of Kenya.
As a highly respected community leader, Moody was responsible for enabling the first Black nurse to train in Britain. During the Second World War, thousands of Black workers and soldiers came to Britain from Africa and the Caribbean, and this increased the workload of the LCP, but it did give the organisation greater purpose and influence.

Dr. Moody was frequently called upon to advise government departments. At the 1944 London conference of the LCP, a 'Charter for Coloured Peoples' was drawn up. It demanded 'full self-government' for the colonies and insisted that racial discrimination in Britain be made illegal: "The same economic, educational, legal and political rights shall be enjoyed by all persons, male and female, whatever their colour. All discrimination in employment, in places of public entertainment and refreshment, or in other public places, shall be illegal and shall be punished." The charter foreshadowed the resolutions of 1945 Pan-African Congress in Manchester.

During the Second World War, five of Dr. Moody's six children received army or RAF commissions. In 1940 his son, Charles, born at 111 King's Road in Peckham, became the first Black officer in the British Army during the Second World War when he joined the Queen's Own Royal West Kent Regiment. Dr. Moody had protested to the Colonial Secretary about the 'colour bar' that existed in the armed services. As a result, the government relaxed the rules regarding voluntary enlistment and emergency commissions. Charles served in the Infantry and the Artillery in England and Africa, then in Italy and finally in Egypt, where he became a Major in 1945. At the end of the war he settled in Jamaica with B Company of the Caribbean Regiment. Charles Moody became a Colonel in 1961, and was awarded an OBE in 1966 as the first Commanding Officer of the Jamaican Territorial Army.

Dr. Moody's son Ronald served in the RAF. His daughter Christine, and son Harold, both qualified as doctors and joined the Royal Army Medical Corps. They became captain and major respectively. His youngest son, Garth, was a pilot-cadet in the RAF.

On December 12, 1940 Dr. Moody went to Buckingham Palace when Her Majesty the Queen received on behalf of Britain a fleet of 35 mobile canteens which had been purchased and provided by the colonies. David A. Vaughan described this important occasion in *Negro Victory* (1950), his biography of Dr. Moody: "During the ceremony Moody was presented to the Queen [who] made enquiries concerning the welfare of the people of his race and displayed a real interest in them." Vaughan also described Moody as "the recognised leader of his people in the Mother Country" and revealed that he "never neglected the easily forgotten small communities of people of African descent domiciled in seaport towns. One such group of 200 lived in Newcastle and were often lonely and unhappy because of their feeling of isolation from the normal social life of the community. In answer to an appeal from them, Moody made a special journey to Newcastle and they derived much benefit and encouragement from his visit."

In 1944 Dr. Moody was one of the first on the scene of the terrible V2 rocket incident in New Cross. Nearly 200 were killed and hundreds injured, mainly mothers and their children among the Christmas shopping crowds. The incident caused the country's heaviest casualties of the war. Dr. Moody attended as part of a team called in from the surrounding area. They struggled night and day amidst the chaos and carnage to bring comfort to the survivors.

Dr. Harold Moody Park (2005)   *Photo: Tim Otway*

A deeply religious man and a lay preacher, for many years Moody held a service of worship at the Camberwell Green Congregational Church in Wren Road where he was a member and deacon. English dignitaries attended these services, the high spot being the singing of spirituals.

Following a strenuous five-month tour of the United States and Caribbean in the winter of 1946-47, Dr. Harold Moody died on April 24, 1947. Thousands of people paid their respects at his funeral which was held at the **Camberwell Green Congregational Church**. Sadly, the church building no longer exists. It was demolished in the 1980s to make way for a block of flats, situated at the back of Camberwell Police Station and Butterfly Walk. The LCP survived him by four years.

In addition to the English Heritage Blue Plaque on 164 Queen's Road (erected in 1995, it is the only English Heritage Blue Plaque in SE15), the park in **Gordon Road, Peckham** has been named after Dr. Moody. In addition to these tributes, on October 31, 2001 an Indian Bean Tree was planted in **Chumleigh Gardens** in **Burgess Park** in memory of Dr. Moody. Speeches were made by the Mayor of Southwark, Russell Profitt (Head of the Peckham Partnership), and Southwark's first Black Mayor, Sam King (see chapter 6). Others in attendance included community activist Linda Bellos and former Southwark Mayor, Councillor Aubyn Graham.

Paul Robeson
and Elisabeth Welch

In the late 1930s the Black American actor and singer Paul Robeson was one of Britain's most popular film personalities. Between 1935 and 1940 he starred in six feature films, and was given top billing in all of them. At the height of his popularity, in 1937, he made a personal appearance at a screening of one of his films at the Elephant and Castle's **Trocadero Cinema**. In 1970 David Shipman described Robeson in *The Great Movie Stars: The Golden Years* as one of the century's great artistes:

> He was successful, but he found the going tough. He had intelligence and fame; was in demand as a concert and recording artist, worked in films and on the stage; but remained always a loner in show business...no singer before or since ever caught the public imagination as Robeson did...no singer before had seemed so real, so unencumbered by artifice, so warm, so sincere: his rich, bass-baritone, whether he sang aria or spiritual, 'spoke' to millions. Today we are accustomed to the singer who 'acts' his lyric; Robeson was virtually the first modern singer, in that the emotion conveyed was as true as the voice. He acted in the same way: powerful, direct, and entirely natural. His few film performances were delightful.

Paul Robeson, born in 1898 in Princeton, New Jersey, may have been one of the most popular stage and screen actors of the 1930s, but he probably suffered more disappointments than any other leading actor of his generation. Black characters in American films of the period rarely moved beyond the white entertainer Al Jolson in blackface, or the dim-witted buffoons played by Black comedy actors like Stepin' Fetchit. For Paul Robeson, an intelligent and progressive actor, there were hardly any opportunities to play challenging roles. Although the characters he played in his British films were generally more dignified than those on offer to him in America, Robeson often found himself in conflict with a film industry that glorified and romanticized the British Empire and colonialism.

Paul Robeson in Song of Freedom (Stephen Bourne)

Robeson and his wife Eslanda settled in London in the 1920s where he enjoyed great success with his appearance as Joe in the stage musical *Show Boat* at the Theatre Royal, Drury Lane. It was in *Show Boat* that he introduced his 'theme' song, 'Old Man River'. Three years earlier, in 1925, the Robesons were befriended by Amanda Ira Aldridge, the London-born daughter of the Black American tragedian, Ira Aldridge (1807-67) (see chapter 2). She presented Robeson with the earrings her father had worn when he played Shakespeare's Othello. She hoped that Robeson would play the role one day. Five years later, at the Savoy Theatre, her wish came true, and Robeson was cast opposite Peggy Ashcroft as Desdemona. He turned to Miss Aldridge for diction and voice training.

When the film producer Alexander Korda decided to bring Edgar Wallace's *Sanders of the River* to the screen, he offered a leading role to Robeson. However, Robeson's association with Korda was not a happy one. During the editing process extra scenes were added, without Robeson's knowledge or approval, glorifying the British Empire and colonialism. Robeson was embarrassed by the version of the film that Korda released to the public, and disowned it, but the contact Robeson made with Africans on the sets of his films had a lasting impact on him, as his son, Paul Robeson Jr, later explained in the Channel 4 television documentary *Songs of Freedom – Paul Robeson and the Black American Struggle* (1986):

> During his film career he met many Africans on the set of films like *Sanders of the River* and *King Solomon's Mines*. Among the extras of *Sanders* was Jomo Kenyatta, the famous burning spear, who then became the first President of Kenya. So culturally he was drawn to the Africans on the set. He found his own African roots, you might say, and became radicalised by the African anti-colonial fighters of that time like Jomo Kenyatta.

In 1936 Robeson co-starred with Elisabeth Welch, another popular Black American singer then working in Britain, in the film *Song of Freedom*. He portrayed a London-born dock worker who acknowledges Africa as his ancestral home and dreams of visiting the continent. This film was important to Robeson because he believed it was the first, he told *Film Weekly* (May 23, 1936): "to give a true picture of many aspects of the life of the coloured man in the west. Hitherto, on the screen, he has been caricatured or presented only as a comedy character. This film shows him as a real man, with problems to be solved, difficulties to be overcome."

Robeson's most outspoken Black critic was Marcus Garvey, the Jamaican nationalist leader who is credited with inspiring Black consciousness on an international scale. In the late 1930s, while residing in London, Garvey denounced Robeson. He strongly objected to the roles Robeson portrayed on stage and screen and, when he left Britain in 1935 to film *Show Boat* in Hollywood, Garvey declared: 'He is gone there to make another slanderous picture against the Negro.'

In 1936 Andre van Gysegham, the left-wing stage director, co-founded the socialist Unity Theatre in London. Unity aimed to provide a showcase for left-wing dramatists. When it opened at new premises on November 25 1937, Robeson took part in the opening ceremony, singing spirituals, and 'Old Man River'. For the latter he altered Oscar Hammerstein II's lyrics from 'tired o'living and scared o'dying' to 'I must keep struggling until I'm dying'. After a long and honourable career as an actor and singer, Robeson announced his strong affiliation to socialism and became one of the most revered and popular figures in the left-wing movement. He gave up a great deal of money to work with the Unity Theatre and his name and personality attracted people who had never been to see a Unity production before.

Robeson also turned his back on concert halls with expensive seats. They generally attracted middle-class audiences. He wanted to reach working-class audiences and succeeded in the autumn of 1937 by making personal appearances at popular music halls as and cinemas. In September 1937, when *King Solomon's Mines* was screened at the **Trocadero Cinema, Elephant and Castle**, Robeson made an appearance at the venue. His presence had a tremendous impact on the lives of the ordinary British public, as recalled almost sixty years later by a Southwark citizen, Joyce

Trocadero, Elephant and Castle, 1935 (Southwark Local History Library)

Neville, in a letter to the author (June 3, 1996). Joyce was a little girl when she attended that historic event at the Trocadero:

> I was born in south London. I loved the cinema – there was not much else to do. At the very small Palace in Southwark Park Road (it used to be called 'The Blue') there was a 'tuppenny rush' for the kids – two in a seat and peanuts crushing on the floor. Friday night was 'talent night' and how we laughed. The **Trocadero Cinema** at the **Elephant and Castle** was a treat. We queued for hours, snaking round the barriers – this is pre-war, of course. I saw all of Paul Robeson's films. His warm personality and magnificent voice made an instantaneous impact. I also saw him 'live' at the Trocadero when he brought the house down (this was between two films). I have never forgotten this performance. He sang for at least an hour, all the favourites. 'Trees', 'Old Man River', 'Deep River', 'Lazybones'. 'The Canoe Song' from *Sanders of the River* was a great favourite, although I believe the film was not one of his own favourites. I enjoyed

The Proud Valley although old films now seem to me to be
very superficial and over-romanticized. They were good in
their day, and some still out, of course.

Robeson was completing his final British film, *The Proud Valley*, when the
Second World War broke out on September 3, 1939. As soon as the
filming ended, he returned to America. *The Proud Valley* enabled
Robeson to express his socialist beliefs and portray the struggles of the
working-class people of South Wales and it stands out from most British
films of its time because it contains believable working-class characters,
not caricatures. After appearing in *The Proud Valley*, Robeson was never
forgotten in South Wales. In the years that the American government
denied him a passport (1950-58), because of his communist sympathies,
the Welsh people were one of the most vocal and active groups who came
to his support.

Robeson symbolised Black consciousness and pride to many Black people,
but ill-health forced him into retirement in the 1960s. He died at the age
of seventy-seven on January 23, 1976 in Philadelphia following a stroke.
In 2002, in the London Borough of Camden, the jazz singer Cleo Laine
unveiled an English Heritage Blue Plaque, bearing Robeson's name, at
The Chestnuts, Branch Hill NW3 where he had lived in 1929-30.

Elisabeth Welch, who co-starred with Paul Robeson in two films, *Song
of Freedom* (1936) and *Big Fella* (1937), remembered him with affection.
In 1985 she sent the following statement to the author:

> It was during the shooting of the film *Song of Freedom* that I
> got to know – and love – Paul Robeson. Arriving to play
> opposite that great man – and it being my first speaking
> part in a film – I was overwhelmed, and as nervous as a
> kitten. The nerves were soon calmed, however, when I saw
> that huge smile light up his face, and felt the warmth of a
> friendly giant when he pressed my hand in both of his, and
> welcomed me. It was a happy time for me, working with
> Paul and watching him work. I found him a man of great

Elisabeth Welch (1946) (Stephen Bourne)

intensity, both in his work and in his beliefs but – thank
goodness – not lacking in humour. We'd sometimes sit
outdoors with our lunch trays, chatting about life and living.
These were times I can never forget. Often he spoke of his
desires and his determination for making a better world
and, as often, we argued as to how it could be achieved.
Once he tried to persuade me to do something for our
people. I had an answer. I'm of mixed blood – African,
American Indian, Scots and Irish. So I said: 'Paul, I belong
to four peoples! I can't make a stand for all of them. You
must excuse me!' And he laughed really hard at that.
Sometimes there was anger in his voice. There was sadness
too. The lunch break over, he'd laugh and say 'to be
continued tomorrow' and back we'd go to the life and lights
of the film studio.

In the 1930s and 1940s Elisabeth Welch was the most famous Black
woman in Britain, rivalled only (from 1939) by another American
expatriate, Adelaide Hall. She was a stylish, sophisticated interpreter of
popular songs, and audiences were drawn to her beauty and elegance,
and her soft, lovely voice. Born in New York in 1904, Elisabeth made
London her home in 1933. In a career that lasted into the 1990s, she
starred in many glamorous West End musicals and revues, in which she
performed songs specially composed for her by the likes of Cole Porter
and Ivor Novello.

The impact Elisabeth has had on other singers is, perhaps, best summed
up by Cleo Laine who, as a child in the 1930s, first heard her singing on
the radio: "I've always admired Elisabeth. Before I came into the business
I used to imitate the way she sang. I loved her voice. When I had the
opportunity to work with her that was a dream come true. Elisabeth has
been a mentor to a lot of singers."

In the 1930s my Aunt Esther (see *Spreading the Word*) made dresses
for Elisabeth. Esther's employer often asked her to deliver them to
Elisabeth's home in Cottage Walk, off Sloane Street. My aunt described

Elisabeth as "a very classy lady. She was a lovely person who always treated me with kindness." Aunt Esther also enjoyed listening to Elisabeth on the radio. In 1934 Elisabeth became the first Black broadcaster to be given her own BBC radio series, *Soft Lights and Sweet Music*. She also made guest appearances in many of the top radio shows of the day, including *Henry Hall's Guest Night, Band Wagon, Monday Night at Eight* and *Workers' Playtime*. She was a particular favourite during the war, and from 1946 to 1950 she made several guest appearances in *Variety Bandbox*, one of the most popular variety shows of the day. It had been launched by the BBC during the war and billed as "bringing the people of variety to a variety of people." It was a fast-moving show with high comedy content. The shows were broadcast live on the Light Programme on Sunday evenings from the **Camberwell Palace of Varieties** in front of live audiences. The *Radio Times* billing for September 17, 1950 confirms that she topped the bill with the comedian Max Wall and Billy Ternent and his Orchestra. Elisabeth sang 'Count Every Star' and 'I Want to Be Loved'. The final *Variety Bandbox* show was broadcast in 1952.

In 1989 Elisabeth was given a special award by the Variety Club of Great Britain for her services to British entertainment. In 1996, at the age of ninety-two, after a career spanning seven decades, Elisabeth decided to call it a day and live quietly in a retirement home in west London. She died at the age of ninety-nine on July 15, 2003.

Sam King

In June 1998, at Southwark Cathedral, Sam King participated in an edition of BBC television's popular Sunday evening series *Songs of Praise*. The programme was broadcast on June 21 as hundreds of churches throughout Britain commemorated the fiftieth anniversary of the arrival of the *Empire Windrush*. In 1948 this ship had brought to Britain the first wave of Caribbean settlers. In all, some 500 people (492 passengers and eight stowaways) landed at Tilbury. Sam was among the *Windrush* passengers interviewed in *Songs of Praise*. Sam had helped to organise the Windrush Foundation to plan the 1998 celebrations. As its Chairman, he personally committed himself to contacting every Black-led church in the country with the message, "It was by the grace of God that we landed, let's praise our God." For Sam, it had been a long and eventful journey that led to him to becoming the first Black Mayor of Southwark, and the first Jamaican to hold the position in Britain. For his services to the community he received an MBE from the Queen in 1998. The journey began in Priestman's River, Jamaica, where he was born on February 20, 1926. Says Sierra Leone-born Columba Blango, who became Mayor of Southwark in 2003: "Sam came to this country at a time when discrimination was at its height, especially in Southwark. He became a great inspiration and role model for a lot of Black people."

The following extracts are taken from interviews with Sam King. They have been found in a variety of sources, which are highly recommended by the author, including the following: *Windrush – The Irresistible Rise of Multi-Racial Britain* (1998) by Mike Phillips and Trevor Phillips; *The Windrush Legacy* (The Black Cultural Archives, 1998); Tony Sewell's *Keep on Moving – The Windrush Legacy* (1998); Marika Sherwood's *Claudia Jones – A Life in Exile* (1999); Rory O'Connell's 1993 interview, available on the Museum of London's *London Voices* website; 'We Interviewed Sam King' from the Windrush Project website by Class 5B, Fairlawn Primary School; and Sam's autobiography *Climbing Up the Rough Side of the Mountain* (1998).

West Indian history versus English history. Sam came from a family of farmers, and says that, at school, he learned very little about the history of the West Indies. Children in the Caribbean were taught British history. As a child, Sam was more likely to learn about Henry VIII and William

Shakespeare, than the Haitian revolutionary Toussaint L'Ouverture, or the Jamaican national hero Paul Bogle, who was hanged in 1865 for leading the Morant Bay rebellion: "I didn't really know Citizen Toussaint exist, just through the local grapevine. Because Haiti is about a hundred and twenty miles off Jamaica...But officially we knew nothing about Citizen Toussaint. We knew nothing about Jamaica history. And I myself have now read Jamaica history, and where they said Paul Bogle became a hero."

Sam King (2004) (South London Press/Georgina Cook)

Religion. Sam explains that religion has played an important part in the lives of people from the Caribbean: "British people ruled the seven seas for about three hundred years. We [in Jamaica] were a colony. We could only ask God for deliverance. We couldn't fight the British navy. If my people talk that it was unjust, the British people would send their gunboat up your river and fire some shots. There were a few good missionaries who thought that slavery was wrong. They were tarred and feathered just before slavery was abolished. Jesus said everybody was equal in the sight of God, so we had to have Christianity or religion to survive. And we did survive. Today only ten per cent of the population in England actively take part in the church. In the West Indies today I

would say seventy-five per cent of the people take active part in religion.
I'm not trying to say that they're better than the English, what I'm trying
to say is, culturally, they look at the Christian side of their survival as the
right thing and God will deliver them. England still assumes that the
British Navy will deliver them. A lot of rubbish."

War. When the Second World War broke out in 1939, Sam was keen to
take part: "I don't think the British Empire was perfect, but it was better
than Nazi Germany. So I wanted to join the armed service. But you could
not because you were from the colony. So I had to do farming. When
England was on the threshold of losing the war, I think they realised they
couldn't beat Nazi Germany, and then they asked 'for God's sakes send
us more planes'. And Jamaica was the first place outside of Britain to put
pennies together, and we collected pennies to buy a squadron of
Spitfires. A lot of people don't realise that." Sam eventually left Jamaica
to join the forces in 1944. Stationed in Britain, he served in the RAF
(Royal Air Force) from 1944 to 1947.

Windrush: Sam returned to Jamaica in 1947, but the men from the
colonies who had served their King and country found their prospects were
bleak: "I being the eldest son should have been a farmer but when I
returned to Jamaica it was shocking. 30,000 of us were thrown back without
any planning, and I decided that my children would not grow up in a
colony because we had no control over education, welfare, health and the
things you produce. They were decided in London markets. So I had no
intention of planting bananas for them at their price. I would rather come
to London or England and work on their term." Sam returned to England
on the *Empire Windrush*: "Caribbean immigration to this country really
started with that boat. To get papers to leave, a Justice of the Peace had to
sign to say you were a responsible citizen and the police had to sign to say
you were not a trouble maker." He left on May 24, 1948, which was Empire
Day, and arrived in Tilbury on June 22: "As we got closer to England there
was great apprehension in the boat because we knew the authorities did
not want us on land. We heard on the BBC news that if there was any
disturbances on the immigrant ship, *HMS Sheffield* would be sent out to
turn us back. So we knew we were not wanted but, being British, once we

arrived at Tilbury everything humanly possible was done to help us."
Many of the arrivals found themselves in Southwark, in temporary
accommodation at the Salvation Army's hostel, and the hostel in Gordon
Road, Peckham: "We from the ex-colonies have contributed a lot to the
improvement of the British way of life. Nearly a third of the inner cities
were destroyed by bombing – we helped to rebuild it."

Father's advice. "My father told me 'whatever the Englishman's tell you,
you must think for yourself'. It's like cricket. Am I going to follow what
the man who ruled me say, or am I going to follow my own survival? My
ancestors been slaves, we survived slavery. We are one of the few people
in the world, the West Indians, who survived slavery. Many Apaches are
brave, not many Apaches are alive now, but we survived. And it was our
intention to survive, and by the grace of God."

Royal Air Force. Sam rejoined the RAF in 1948, and served until 1953:
"When I was wearing the air force uniform there was more respect or
understanding for me. But once I was a civilian out there, it was a harder
life. The people who didn't know me were different."

Camberwell. In the post-war years, settlers from Africa and the Caribbean
faced discrimination when they tried to rent rooms: "You couldn't get a
place to rent. You're a Black man. You have an ad. There's a room for
rent. You go. 'Good afternoon, madam'. Sorry. No Blacks. There's nothing
you can do." Sam sent for his brother, Wilton, and, within a year of him
arriving, they bought their first home in Sears Street, Camberwell. In 1950
they became the second Black family in Southwark to buy their own home:
"Now once we had a home I could come out of the RAF. I was standing on
my own two feet." Sam was still in the Royal Air Force when he applied for
a mortgage but a letter came back saying 'thank you Corporal King for
applying for a mortgage, but since you are from Jamaica, a colony, we
would recommend that you go back to the colony.' Sam took the letter to
the owner who was selling the house in Sears Street. The owner lived off
Camberwell Road: "He was so disgusted. He said 'it's a disgrace. I will give
you the mortgage but you must swear on the Bible that you will pay.' And
he gave us the mortgage, and I don't have to tell you we paid quicker than

the time. He gave us a mortgage for ten years, and we paid it off in five. Because we couldn't get mortgages we pooled our money to help others in the Black community. We called it a 'Partner' and it worked well."

Metropolitan Police. After leaving the RAF in 1953, Sam applied to join the Metropolitan Police. He passed the academic test. He passed the medical. Then he went before a selection board of four Chief Constables, one of whom succeeded in preventing Sam from joining. He brought up the problem of Black RAF personnel who had been at the centre of trouble in Yorkshire when they went to dance halls, and came into conflict with white Americans who raised objections to them dancing with white women: "He's trying to say we are unlawful. I went home and about three days after a letter came from the Commissioner of the Metropolitan Police saying he was very sorry but they will not have me. He didn't give any reason. I was totally disappointed." It took until 1967 for the Metropolitan Police to appoint its first Black police officer: Norwell Roberts. He served for thirty years, and in 1996 he was honoured with the Queen's Police Medal for distinguished service.

Post Office. Sam worked on a building site, and did some painting work, but his aim was to find a stable and permanent job. He was eventually taken on by the Post Office, where he stayed until he retired: "When I started a Black man could not get into the Post Office unless he was an ex-serviceman. It wasn't easy. There were barriers everywhere and my people suffered terrible humiliation." On June 26, 1954 Sam married Mavis (Mae) Kirlew, a student nurse, at Emmanuel Church which was situated on Camberwell Road and Blucher Road. In 1963 it was closed and later demolished to make way for a block of flats called Bishopsmead.

Claudia Jones. Sam became involved in community affairs in the middle 1950s, and befriended Claudia Jones, one of the most important Black community leaders in Britain at that time. Born in Trinidad, Claudia's family moved to Harlem, New York, where the young Claudia became a leading figure in Communist and Black politics. Forced into exile in Britain in 1955, Claudia arrived in London penniless and friendless. She became active in civil rights campaigns amongst the new Black Caribbean communities, and in March 1958 she launched a monthly Black newspaper, the Brixton-based *West Indian Gazette*. Claudia was the editor, and Sam was the circulation manager. Sam described her as a 'no nonsense' person: "Her conversations ranged widely from social and political science to jurisprudence and theology, and they were solid, instructive and interesting with the minimum of humour. The retentiveness of her memory was enviable as one listened to the anecdotes of her life."

Community support. In the middle 1950s Sam joined the Labour Party and got together with other Caribbean settlers to assist and support newcomers. They were allotted different areas and Sam was allotted Camberwell, and part of his responsibility was to help, support and advise new settlers. Oswald Mosley's fascists were very active at the time: "They were active in Peckham and my friend, Gold Teeth Stanford, was in charge in Peckham. It could have been a real hot spot but he did a good job. Brixton was a flash point, but once Claudia Jones goes down Brixton Road and says something, that was as good as carried."

Riots of 1958. Sam's advice was needed after the Notting Hill riots of 1958. Some West Indians were planning to have a party in Albany Road, Camberwell: "And they came to me and asked me if they should have the party and I said 'no, we are in England and we are free but at present we've just had the Notting Hill riot. Cancel it.' If they'd had the party at that time, some fascist or teddy boys come and give trouble. And give Jamaicans their due, they are not afraid to die. And the teddy boys and skinheads know that."

Carnival. Claudia was instrumental in organising an annual indoor event to showcase the talents and culture of Britain's Black Caribbean communities. In November 1958, just a few months after the Notting Hill riots, a Caribbean Carnival Committee was set up under the sponsorship of the *West Indian Gazette*. The Committee must have worked swiftly and efficiently, since on January 30, 1959 it was able to mount what was announced as the Caribbean Carnival, at St. Pancras Town Hall in central London. The carnival was organised by the *West Indian Gazette*, and the carnival cabaret was directed by the popular Trinidadian folk singer and actor, Edric Connor: "The West Indian carnival started in 1959 because after the Notting Hill riot, Claudia Jones thought that the media, especially the right-wing media, were not very helpful or were more negative towards us. Therefore through the *West Indian Gazette* she decided that we should have a carnival to let the nation and our people see that we can contribute something in the community. By the grace of God fourteen people attended the first committee meeting for the carnival." The early events took place in halls but by the time of Claudia's death in 1964, it had taken to the streets and developed into an annual event called the Notting Hill Carnival.

Dr. Martin Luther King. In 1964 Dr. Martin Luther King, passing through London on his way to Oslo to collect his Nobel Peace Prize, called to see Claudia Jones at the offices of the *West Indian Gazette* in Brixton. She had been working in America before Dr King was imprisoned in Little Rock: "They said, 'all right, Sam will make the tea because Sam is a reliable person If you tell Sam to make the tea, get the sugar, it will be done'. I gave Dr Martin Luther King a cup of tea."

National Front in Peckham. The National Front marched through Peckham several times in the 1970s and early 1980s, and these contributed to the tensions that led to the 1981 Brixton and Peckham uprisings. The uprisings had an enormous impact on community relations. In those days Southwark did not have a police and community consultative group, so it was left to community leaders like Sam to take responsibility for mediating between the community and the police: "The police commander used to contact me and a few others. We go and have a meeting and we told him that if you let the National Front march through Peckham I can't stop the people burning it down. If you stop them from marching through Peckham you will have no problem with the Rastafarians. Went up Peckham Road, saw some fellow, he said, 'Mr King what happens'. I said 'ah now, hear this, we've got a problem. The National Front said they are marching through here, the commander of Peckham police have given his word that they will not march'. But as long as the National Front do not walk through Peckham High Street, we are going to behave ourself. Another fellow say 'Mr King is all right, he's been around a bit and if he said there's no problem, there's no problem'. You always have individuals who wants to rush up front. I was never one to rush up front, but when there were problems somehow I always be there."

Labour councillor. For the local elections of 1982, Sam was selected as a Labour councillor for Bellenden ward: "I had to do some canvassing and from the reception I was getting on the door steps I was convinced that the voting was going my way, but I took nothing for granted. I received much help and encouragement from colleagues and well-wishers and when the voting was declared I won with an overwhelming majority. I dropped almost all my other commitments and concentrated on serving the Bellenden ward and the people of Southwark."

Mayor of Southwark. There were other Black councillors, including Aubyn Graham (later the Mayor of Southwark in 1995-96), but Sam was the first to be elected the Mayor of Southwark: "My first reaction was that there were bright people around – why me?" In mid-April 1983, at a meeting of the Labour group, a proposition was put forward for Sam to become the next mayor of Southwark. There were forty-six members present in the council room entitled to vote, and three names went forward. Sam won on the first ballot with over seventy-five per cent of the votes cast: "Recollections of my life came flooding in, calming the situation on the *Windrush*, setting up saving schemes, buying houses – ha! These were the training grounds for a position I never had the audacity to envisage, let alone hold. I managed to summon some courage, rose to my feet and accepted the mayorship." Sam said he felt very glad and proud to be mayor: "It was a brilliant opportunity. It was not easy. People thought that Black people could not be mayors. One day I was invited to seven different institutions and I had to speak five times. But on the whole I found it to be a pleasant experience." Sam retired as a councillor in 1986, settled in Bexley, and became a leader in the Pentecostal Church.

Threats. However, just before Sam took up the post, something unpleasant happened: "A month before I became the mayor the National

Front in Southwark telephoned my home to say that if I take up the appointment they would burn down my house and slit my throat. I telephoned Peckham police and they said 'no, they might be somebody making a joke or something'. They were not interested. About seven o'clock a policeman did arrive. Very reluctant, took my name. He says 'you're not to worry about it because nobody would really do that. It's a joke'. Within ten minutes the telephone rang again, I said [to the police officer] 'excuse me, can you answer the telephone'. He answered the telephone. He was shocked. He telephoned his office and within one hour there was a policeman outside my door."

BBC TV. Sam says the greatest satisfaction he had during his term of office as Mayor was appearing on BBC television in an edition of *Songs of Praise*, recorded at Southwark Cathedral in February 1984: "My cup ran over with joy as the uninhibited Black choirs exploded with pulsating vitality in the presence of an overflowing cathedral and ten million viewers. I was the coordinator, the link man drawing together thirty Pentecostal churches which stood and delivered in the most spectacular manner." On June 15, 1988 Sam made another television appearance, also for the BBC, in the popular tea-time chat show, *Wogan*. The occasion was the fortieth anniversary of the arrival of *Windrush*, and Sam was interviewed by the host, Terry Wogan, with fellow passenger Vince Reid. Ten years later, on May 30, 1998, Sam was featured in the first edition of *Windrush*, the BBC's landmark, four-part television series. Around this time, Sam made the following observation: "For every third of the average English people who are unreasonable to us there is another third who will go out of their way to help you. The other third couldn't care less one way or the other as long as their football team plays on Saturday and they can get beer in the pubs."

When Denzel and *Desmond's* came to Peckham

FOR QUEEN AND COUNTRY

A number of films and television programmes have been based in Peckham. Some of them have even used the area as a location. In 1988 the Hollywood star Denzel Washington came to south east London to star in *For Queen and Country*, but the tradition of importing American actors to play important Black roles in British films has always been controversial. The most famous examples are Sidney Poitier in *To Sir, With Love* (1967) and Forest Whitaker in *The Crying Game* (1992). This practice has always upset qualified Black British actors who were passed over in favour of their American counterparts. Americans have always been considered more 'glamorous' and thus able to draw audiences into cinemas. Denzel was cast over a number of qualified Black British actors, including Gary McDonald, who told the *Caribbean Times* (February 17-23, 1989): "I was supposed to be doing that film. I worked on it for about four weeks and joined the Territorial Army so that I could actually become the part". Gary lost the part because Americans were putting up most of the money and they wanted an actor their audience could recognise. Gary said: "I was gutted. If a

Denzel Washington in For Queen and Country (1988) (UIP)

black actor from this country had been used it would really help get things moving for us here".

The director of *For Queen and Country*, Martin Stellman, co-authored the screenplay with a young Black writer, Trix Worrell, and Denzel was cast as Reuben, a disillusioned Falklands' war hero. After leaving the British army, because they refused to give him promotion, Reuben returns home to south east London to face more racism, and an urban war. No particular area is identified in the film. The council estate could have been in Brixton, Peckham or Deptford. But some journalists assumed that the **North Peckham** estate was the location for the film, with its grim, claustrophobic walkways, and sense of danger. Writer S. I. Martin (see Southwark Connections) remembers some of the filming taking place in **Keston House** in **Walworth's Kinglake Street**, near the **Old Kent Road**. "The guy whose flat they used still lives there," he says.

ONLY FOOLS AND HORSES

At the time *For Queen and Country* was released, another Denzel – Denzil – was being featured as a regular supporting character in the popular BBC television comedy series *Only Fools and Horses*. Denzil has been played by Liverpool's Paul Barber since the award-winning series was launched in 1981. The character has become a familiar face in the comic adventures of the Trotter brothers, Del (David Jason) and Rodney (Nicholas Lyndhurst), who live in a high-rise council flat in Nelson Mandela House. In the 1980s, *Only Fools and Horses* put Peckham on the map, as far as television comedy was concerned, and the series became a national favourite. Says Mark Lewisohn in *Radio Times Guide to TV Comedy* (1998): "The final and perhaps most abiding memory is that of the dilapidated vehicle that served as the Trotters' company transport: an ancient yellow Reliant Robin three-wheeler with the legend – one that encapsulated Del's entire business philosophy – 'New York, Paris, Peckham'." Paul Barber played leading roles in two other situation comedies of the 1980s: *The Front Line* and *The Brothers McGregor*, but he is best-known for his role of Mr Horse in the film *The Full Monty* (1997).

DESMOND'S

Another popular sit-com based in **Peckham** was *Desmond's* (1989-94).
A Peckham barber's shop at 204 Bellenden Road was the basis for this
series which was first seen on Channel 4 on January 5, 1989. It was created
by Trix (*For Queen and Country*) Worrell, who had been born in St Lucia but
raised in Peckham. Remembering the Bellenden Road barber's shop from
his youth, Worrell formulated the basis for a sitcom which he successfully
pitched to television comedy producer Humphrey Barclay. Its wry humour
came from the attitudinal differences between the Guyanese settler,
Desmond Ambrose (Norman Beaton), and his British-born children.
Desmond has been described as a Black Victor Meldrew (*One Foot in the
Grave*) and a traditionalist. Carmen Munroe played his loving and
supportive wife, Shirley. Worrell was also keen to highlight the differences
between Africans and Caribbeans so viewers were exposed to racism
between, for example, the African student Matthew (Gyearbuour Asante),
and the Caribbean characters, especially Porkpie (Ram John Holder).

*Desmond's (1989) (from left to right) Geff Francis, Trix Worrell, Kim Walker, Norman Beaton,
Carmen Munroe and Justin Pickett (Channel 4)*

73

Desmond's lasted for six series, ending on December 19, 1994. Six days earlier its star, Norman Beaton, had died at the age of sixty while visiting Guyana, the land of his birth. His co-star, Carmen Munroe, once described *Desmond's*: "We have successfully created a space for ourselves, where we can just be a real, honest, loving family, with problems like lots of people, and we can present that with some degree of truth and still not lose the comedy." In 1998 the Royal Television Society presented a Silver Medal to *Desmond's* "to mark the fiftieth anniversary of Windrush."

WE THE RAGAMUFFIN
We the Ragamuffin, a 30-minute musical drama set around a group of real 'ragamuffins' living on the "no go" North Peckham estate, couldn't have been further away from *Desmond's* in its portrayal of young Black life on our streets. Shown on Channel 4 on September 7, 1992, its director Julian Henriques, and producer Russell Newell, filmed *We the Ragamuffin* in the miles of raised walkways and corridors of the North Peckham estate that gave access to the flats with virtually no shops or other facilities. When the estate was built in the 1970s, the developers and architects won awards. Soon afterwards, the estate deteriorated to the point where, on some walkways, there were more flats burnt out than occupied. It has since been demolished to make way for new housing. Said Lorraine Grifffiths in *The Weekly Journal* (November 5, 1992): "*We the Ragamuffin* bravely attempts new innovations in British television...Interweaving a gritty realism with the fantasy of the musical genre, the film is as humorous as it is elucidating. Like a mirror image of the community itself, Ragamuffin carries the simple message: music is a powerful and social force."

NEWTON I. ADUAKA AND RAGE
When nineteen-year-old Newton I. Aduaka arrived in Peckham from Nigeria in 1985, he saw the city as one of possibilities, "And then I saw how depressed my surroundings were and my ideas changed very quickly. I started to experience racism which was something I wasn't used to. At first it was little things. You hear people talk. Then you become aware of people disliking you. I'd get on a bus, and a white woman would grab her bag. And you realise what that means. But I also found racism

74

between young Africans and Caribbeans. Life's a funny thing, because someone always has to be the underdog. So, for me, it was a very strange situation to suddenly find myself a second-class citizen."

Newton trained at the London International Film School, and in his feature film *Rage* (1999) he wanted to tell a story about teenagers: "and deal with multiculturalism by casting a Black kid, a white kid and a mixed race kid in a real life setting. I chose Peckham. I lived on the North Peckham estate for four years, and that was my first experience of living in London. Total neglect. And it felt right to make *Rage* there."

Rage explores the lives of three youths in contemporary London where cultures, class, race and sexuality intermingle and influence each other freely, and adopted American street style is the fashion of the day. The three teenagers are mixed race Jamie (aka 'Rage'), a rebellious rapper played by Fraser Ayres, Godwin ('G'), an introverted Black gay pianist, played by Shaun Parkes, and white Thomas ('T'), a forlorn DJ in search of a cause, played by John Pickard.

The support for *Rage* came from the people, from the audience. In Britain, the London Film Festival screened it in 1999. The Black Filmmaker International Film Festival in 2000. It was screened at the Ritzy in Brixton and the Peckham Premiere. In 2001 Aduaka took the film to festivals in Toronto, Los Angeles, Burkino Faso, Milan and India. That same year Aduaka received an award as Best Director of a First Feature at the Pan African Film Festival in Los Angeles, and soon afterwards he was honoured with the Oumarou Ganda Prize for Director of a First Feature at FESPACO, the Pan-African Film Festival of Ouagadougou.

Aduaka says: "I have no right to judge anyone. I want to make other films like *Rage* that are non-judgemental. To highlight the problems we have in human nature, of man's injustice and hypocrisy to others. I want to deal with this, and fight this, in cinema. That is my chosen field. We have to get out of this state of mind where we think this island and its narrow-minded executives who run the film industry is all there is. They have a British Empire mentality. There's a world out there."

Marianne Jean-Baptiste

When the Camberwell-born actress Marianne Jean-Baptiste received
a Best Supporting Actress Oscar nomination in 1996 for her role in Mike
Leigh's critically acclaimed film *Secrets and Lies*, she could reasonably
have expected to achieve star status in this country. After all, she was the
first British-born Black actress to have been nominated. However, when
Marianne became the focus of media attention at the time of the Cannes
Film Festival in 1997, it was not because she had landed a major role in
a film, but for making accusations of racism. Within months of receiving
Oscar, BAFTA (British Academy of Film and Television Arts) and Golden
Globe nominations, the actress complained that she had been excluded
from a celebration attended by Britain's newest film personalities. Simon
Perry, chief executive of British Screen, had invited a group of young
actors, including Emily Watson and Kate Winslet, to the Cannes Film
Festival, but there were no Black actors on the list. In *The Guardian* (May
15, 1997), Marianne complained:

> When I was told that British Screen had invited a group of
> young actors out to Cannes, I just burst into tears because
> I thought this is so unfair. It was a snub. What more do they
> want? If you think about it, I made history. Not only was
> I the first black British woman to be nominated for an
> Oscar, I was the first black British person. I see myself as
> British and I want to be celebrated by Britain [...] I don't
> want to sound like someone who has a chip on their
> shoulder. But if you keep quiet nothing will ever change
> and nothing will ever be done about it.

Marianne also criticised the "old men" who run the British film industry
whom, she said: "just have not got a clue. They've got to come to terms
with the fact that Britain is no longer a place where people ride horses,
wear long frocks and drink tea. The national dish is no longer fish and
chips, it's curry."

Since that time, apart from her memorable portrayal of Doreen
Lawrence in the 1999 television film *The Murder of Stephen Lawrence*,
British producers have ignored Marianne. Since her 'outburst', it seems
Marianne is being punished for speaking her mind.

•

Born in **St. Giles's Hospital, Camberwell** on April 26, 1967, and raised
on a **Peckham** council estate, Marianne inherited her surname from her
father, Felix, who is half Saint Lucian-half French. He worked for a
marquee-hire firm. Her mother, Drucilla, who came from Antigua,
worked in an old people's home, and did not want her daughter to attend
the local 'rough' school. She persuaded Marianne to try for a grammar
school instead. When Marianne first attended Southwark's **St. Saviour's
and St. Olave's School** in the **New Kent Road**, she was taunted by other
kids, but, she later reflected: "if they gave me any trouble I gave it straight
back. But because I was little they thought I must be really tough or really
mad. On both counts they didn't really want to mess with me."

In her spare time, Marianne was a regular user of the **North Peckham
Library** in **Old Kent Road**, and attended classes at a Black-run Saturday
morning school, as well as local community drama classes. "In the 1970s
there was all this help the poor stuff," she recalled, "so I used to go to
things like the **Southwark Children's Theatre** workshop." Marianne
originally planned to become a barrister, but chose acting instead. Her
father told her: "Whatever you do, make sure you do it well."

Marianne went to RADA (Royal Academy of Dramatic Art), and said:
"My three years at RADA were great. I worked every night as an
usherette at the Empire, Leicester Square. I knew why I wanted to go to
RADA and it wasn't for a social life. I knew I needed to read about the
different styles of theatre. I suppose it says something about insecurity
as I didn't want anybody to say something about theatre I wouldn't
understand, or mention a name I didn't know." After leaving RADA in
1990, Marianne worked with a couple of theatre companies, Temba and
Cheek By Jowl, for whom she gave an acclaimed performance as Mariana
in Shakespeare's *Measure for Measure* in 1994.

There was a small role in the film *London Kills Me* (1991) and occasional
television appearances in drama series like *Cracker* (1994). On stage she
was directed by Mike Leigh in *It's a Great Big Shame* at the Theatre Royal,
Stratford East, in 1993, and they hit it off immediately. He cast her as the
optometrist Hortense, an adoptee who goes in search of her biological

Marianne Jean-Baptiste and Brenda Blethyn in Secrets and Lies (1996) (British Film Institute)

mother, in his film *Secrets and Lies*. Critics raved about Marianne's performance. Said Mansel Stimson in *Gay Times* (June 1996): "The heroine is Hortense, beautifully realised by Marianne Jean-Baptiste." However, creating Hortense under Leigh's direction demanded a great deal of emotional energy and professional perseverance, as the actress explained to Gary Younge in *The Guardian* (March 12, 1997):

> You have to create the whole character. All of their
> emotions have to be organic. I went to City University for
> three months to do optometry. I had to work out what sort
> of school she would go to and what the walk from the bus
> stop to the school would be. When people meet me they
> expect to meet Hortense, which is great because I love her.
> She has such a warmth and generosity and ability to think
> things through.

Following *Secrets and Lies*, work for Marianne seemed to dry up. After spending time on the dole, and writing the music for Mike Leigh's film *Career Girls* (1997), she decided to pack her bags and try her luck in America. There were several supporting roles in film and television dramas, including *Oprah Winfrey Presents: The Wedding* (1998) with Halle Berry, *A Murder of Crows* (1999) with Cuba Gooding Jr, and *Spy Game* (2001) with Robert Redford and Brad Pitt.

In Britain, Marianne was cast opposite Lenny Henry in a BBC television comedy-drama *The Man* (1999), and as Doreen Lawrence in the television film *The Murder of Stephen Lawrence*, first shown on ITV on February 18, 1999. This drama documentary followed events from the murder of Stephen on April 22, 1993, right up to the present, through the eyes of his parents. Marianne's outstanding performance earned her praise from the critics and a Royal Television Society Best Actress nomination. She told Paul Macey in *The Voice* (February 15, 1999):

> It was important for me to do the film of an important real-life, high profile incident such as this, as it served as a real eye-opener to all the nonsense, cover-up and runaround the family have faced. Of course I knew about the case before, but I have now got a true sense of what the family went through and how important this case is for them and a lot of other people. The film helps to bring home that it could be any one of us. Stephen was killed for the sole reason that he was Black and he wasn't given justice for this. Both Doreen and Neville were very supportive throughout the making of the film. I talked a lot with Doreen in particular. She is a very private person and you have to respect the fact that she never wanted to be in the public spotlight but was open and answered lots of the questions I had to ask her. I found the filming traumatic. We went to shoot in the Well Hall Road and when I saw the plaque [to mark the spot of the murder] my breathing started to change. And then when I walked the distance Stephen had to cover when running from the attack it really got to me.

The Murder of Stephen Lawrence won the BAFTA for Best Television Drama but, regrettably, Marianne was overlooked in the Best Actress category. BAFTA members didn't even nominate her. However, the film's writer and director, Paul Greengrass, did pay tribute to the actress in his acceptance speech.

Since its premiere on American television on September 26, 2002, the critically acclaimed drama series *Without a Trace* has given Marianne a huge profile. Her regular appearances as Vivian Johnson, the no-nonsense investigator attached to the Missing Persons Squad of the Federal Bureau of Investigation (FBI), has established her as one of the first Black British actresses to find success in America. The fast-paced series, starring Anthony LaPaglia as senior agent Jack Malone, and produced by CBS, has also been shown with equal success in Britain, on Channel 4. Marianne told Mikey Massive in *New Nation* (May 3, 2004): "In the States, an Oscar nomination makes it much easier to get work. In the UK I am still being asked to meet for initial discussions about roles." But what is there to discuss? Marianne's ability is no secret. This actress is a star.

Rio Ferdinand

The football career of Rio Ferdinand has gone from strength to strength, but Peckham's local hero has never forgotten where he's from. Although he is one of the major stars of the world of football, Rio still finds time to visit community projects in Peckham, and provides young people with much-needed sports equipment. He has taken talented youngsters for trials to various football clubs, and paid their expenses. "The work I have done with local kids is something that comes naturally," he told Laura Francis in *Southwark Life* in 2003. "I feel I can give something back and encourage kids to live their dreams like I'm doing."

However, Rio is not the first sporting hero to be connected to Southwark. In the early 1920s the Manchester-born boxer and political activist Len Johnson (1902-1974) was ranked among Britain's top six middleweights. By 1925 Johnson was firmly established as one of Britain's leading boxers. Before retiring from the ring in 1933, Johnson made many appearances at **The Ring**, a popular boxing arena in **Blackfriars Road**. In 1923 Johnson made his London debut at the venue, and some of his greatest fights took place there. His biographer, Michael Herbert, described his most famous fight in *Never Counted Out! The Story of Len Johnson, Manchester's Black Boxing Hero and Communist* (1992): "Perhaps Len's most famous fight at this venue was on 13 February 1928, when he met Jack Hood over twenty rounds. The Prince of Wales and Douglas Fairbanks Junior were in the audience to see Len defeated on points. During the intervals, the Prince apparently briefly sampled working-class life with a cup of tea at a local café."

Towards the end of the Second World War, Johnson joined the Communist Party, and remained a member until his death. Along with C. L. R. James, George Padmore, Jomo Kenyatta, and other Black radicals, he was involved in the Pan-African Congress held in Manchester in 1945. Len spoke at various left-wing meetings with Paul Robeson (see chapter 5) and during the 1950s he visited Russia. Says Gary Shaw in *Oxford Dictionary of National Biography* (2004): "Although Johnson's communist affiliations make him almost unique among British sportsmen, it is his boxing career for which he is most famous. He was one of only a handful of highly talented Black British boxers active before the Second World War, and was probably the

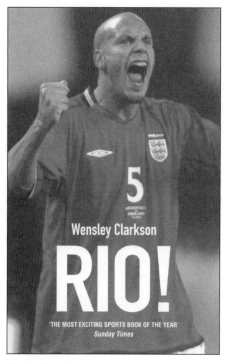

Rio Ferdinand

most skilful Black British boxer until the emergence of Randolph (Randy) Turpin in the early 1950s. He met all the leading British and European boxers of his day, and defeated most of them. However, owing to the colour bar in British boxing, which was lifted by the time Turpin came to the fore, he was unable to contest a British title, even though many contemporaries, including boxing journalists, rated him as the best middleweight in Europe about 1925-28."

Born in Jamaica in 1960, boxing champion Lloyd Honeyghan came to Britain with his family in 1969 and was raised in **Bermondsey** and on the **Brandon Estate**. Turning professional in 1980, Honeyghan captured the British, Commonwealth and European welterweight titles before achieving a totally unexpected victory over America's Donald Curry in Atlantic City in 1986. Honeyghan became the undisputed world champion and Southwark gave him a hero's welcome. He relinquished the WBA and IBF titles before losing the WBC title to Mexican Jorge Vaca in 1987. Lloyd regained the title from Vaca within five months but finally lost it to an American, Marlon Starling, in Las Vegas in 1989. Lloyd hated the big-talking Starling 'more than any other guy I've fought' but he still shook hands with the new champion and congratulated him. "We're all warriors in that ring," said Lloyd, "we're all brothers. He's a brave man." Ken Gorman described Lloyd in *40 Boxers Describe My Greatest Fight* (1996) as: "one of the greatest fighters this country has ever produced, a champion whose heart was bigger than his ego."

Chris Eubank is another boxing champion with links to Southwark. Born in East Dulwich in 1966 to Jamaican parents, he moved away from the area with his family immediately after he was born, but returned to Southwark when he was eleven. He went to **Bellenden Junior School** before moving on to **Thomas Carlton Secondary**. With a reputation that he later described as "boisterous", young Christopher was suspended from school eighteen times, and eventually sent to **Peckham Manor Secondary School**. Expelled from Peckham Manor, he ended up in care, living in various institutions around south east London including Karib, a care home for Black minority ethnic youth, in **Nunhead**, and **Davey Street** in Peckham.

Eventually Chris found himself living on the streets, and surviving by shoplifting. As he later explained in his autobiography, *Chris Eubank* (2003): "I had been so unruly when I visited my father on leave from the care homes, he could not tolerate my behaviour and eventually refused to have me back home at all. For the next eighteen months, I was homeless. My territory was around **Peckham** and **Walworth Road**. I did not have a permanent roof over my head. Much has been made in the media, and indeed by the public I meet, about how awful this must have been. No, I won't have this said. I lived like a king…About once a week I would not be able to get a floor for the night, so I would break into a car and sleep on the back seat. I spent many a happy night napping on car seats in **Peckham, Camberwell** or the **Elephant and Castle**…Everyone's burden is heaviest. I prefer to look at things this way. If I look at it any other way, it gives people who are less fortunate an excuse to say the world owes them something – it doesn't. *The world owes you nothing*. If I had looked at my younger years in that way, I would have suffocated in resentment. I could not allow that, I had things to do. I had to fly, so to speak…I headed for a new life which was waiting for me in New York. My flight was on 29 November 1982."

Moving to America, Chris launched a boxing career which led him to playing a major role in the golden era of British middleweight boxing in the 1990s. Having taken part in, and won, some of the most brutal fights in British boxing history, Chris eventually retired from the boxing ring.

He has since enjoyed the life of a celebrity, appearing in such popular television shows as *Celebrity Big Brother* and *At Home With the Eubanks*. Interviewed by Zoe Walker in the *South London Press* in 2004, he reflected on his youth: "There was too much temptation for me. And I fell into the trap of doing the stupid thing, which was to shoplift, smoke, drink, and get suspended from school. It was tough, because I didn't understand that I shouldn't follow people and I didn't have things to occupy my time."

Born in King's College Hospital, Lambeth, the West Ham and England football champion Rio Ferdinand lived in **Gisburn House** on the **Friary Estate** in Peckham for eighteen years. "Growing up on the Friary Estate was great. There was always something happening and I was very happy there," he says. He attended **Camelot Primary School** in Peckham and spent his leisure time in various local venues, including **Leyton Gardens Adventure Playground, Peckham Leisure Centre, North Peckham Library** and **Peckham Rye Park**. He also belonged to a drama club at the **Peckham Settlement**. His early interest in gymnastics led to being named Inner London Schoolboy Champion, but at the age of eleven he started playing football seriously. He later recalled: "I first started playing football on the Peckham estate where I grew up with all my mates. There were some grass fields nearby and we were always there, at weekends, after school. We'd be out there playing for hours. I was always playing football around the house. I was always getting told off for knocking things over and breaking ornaments! I was a nightmare. I used to really look up to attacking footballers when I was younger. Players like Maradona and Ian Wright were amazing to watch because you knew something would always happen when they got the ball. I grew up watching these players and wanted to play like them."

As a schoolboy, Rio's talents were tested at Queen's Park Rangers and Middlesborough before he signed for West Ham at the age of fifteen. He stayed there until he joined Leeds United in November 2000 and, on July 22, 2002, came his momentous signing from Leeds United to Manchester United for £30 million – officially making him the world's most expensive defender at the time.

Rio has never lost touch with Peckham and through his frequent visits to the area and involvement in the Damilola Taylor Trust he has encouraged many of Southwark's youth to strive to better themselves. As a local lad who has risen to the heights of a career in international football, Rio has become a popular and influential role model for young people. Rio was a strong ally and friend to Southwark during the aftermath of Damilola Taylor's tragic death. He recorded a personal appeal for young people to come forward with information about anything they might have seen or heard and was the first contributor to the Damilola Taylor Trust in which he has maintained an interest ever since.

In 2002 he told the *Evening Standard*: "I love Peckham. It's like, my place. When I was young and went to school outside Peckham, you made sure everyone knew where you came from."

In 2003 Rio was honoured with a Southwark Council Blue Plaque. It overlooks the adventure playground in Peckham's Leyton Square.

Southwark Connections

Lack of space has prevented the inclusion of a number of outstanding Black citizens and organisations who are – or have been – active in the Southwark community in recent years. The following list acknowledges some of them.

Sandra Agard is a popular writer and storyteller who has organised live literature events at Peckham Library for many years. Sandra particularly likes reading the stories which feature the mischievous spider Anansi. These stories were carried to the Caribbean by slaves from Africa. She says, "I began telling stories to my family, then to my classmates. In plays I use my African, Caribbean and Black British experience to inform my work. I use the orator tradition and this has an enormous effect on audiences." One of Sandra's most successful one-woman shows is *Louisa Grant tells the story of her sister Mary Seacole* which she presented at a number of venues in Southwark, including several libraries, throughout 2005.

Segun Akindayini came to London from Nigeria in 1978. He is credited with developing the concept of the African Video Centre from a home-based business (mail order only) to the formation of Britain's first and largest stocks of African, Caribbean and Black Hollywood films. He opened the first African video shop in Southwark at the Elephant and Castle Shopping Centre in 1993. He told the *Southwark News* in 2005: "Southwark is a nice place to live – the crowd, the friendly inhabitants. Southwark is really improving, with all the regeneration programmes. Southwark Council is looking at the safety of people. My video shop is working ok. A lot more people are coming in, not just Black people, but white and foreigners too. They're watching African films. Southwark is cosmopolitan."

Patrick Augustus, musician and author, was born and raised in Southwark. In 2001 his bestselling novel *Babyfather* became one of BBC television's first Black drama series. Says Patrick, "The Ku Klux Klan had a saying that if you want to hide something from a Black man, put it in a book, and I noticed that me and my friends weren't reading as much as we should. So I took the advice of Marcus Garvey who said we need to write our own stories. I'd always be listening to my friends crying about trying to get access to their children – so *Babyfather* came out."

Linda Bellos was born in London, the daughter of a Nigerian father and a Polish/Jewish mother. She has been actively involved in grass roots community activism for over thirty years. In 1981 Linda became the first Black woman and the first Black lesbian to join the *Spare Rib* feminist collective. In the 1980s she gained public recognition as part of the Greater London Council's Women's Unit, and as vice-chair of the local Labour Party's Black Section. Committed to lesbian politics since 1980, Linda was an organiser for the first Black lesbian conference in Britain, *Zami 1*, in 1985. Also, from 1985, she became a councillor in the London Borough of Lambeth and from 1986 to 1988 she was leader of Lambeth Council. After working in local government, Linda started a career as a freelance management consultant and writer. As a community adviser to the Metropolitan Police, Linda has co-chaired the Lesbian, Gay, Bisexual, Transgender (LGBT) Advisory Group and, from 1999-2003, chaired Southwark's Anti-Homophobic Forum. In 2002, partly for her work as an adviser to the murder investigation of Damilola Taylor, Linda received a Metropolitan Police Volunteer Award. Linda is currently chair of SAVO (Southwark Action for Voluntary Organisations). In 2000, Linda wrote movingly about her father in an essay entitled *Age* in *IC3 – The Penguin Book of New Black Writing in Britain*: "I wonder what this society will look like when a generation of Black people born here have parents and grandparents from whom to learn and from whom advice and guidance can be gained. I know that such a sense of continuity did not exist for my father or for many others from Africa and the Caribbean. They made do without Grey Heads, but they retained the memory of them back home. It is we who grew up here in the 1950s, 1960s and 1970s who did not have that benefit and may not have noticed it was missing. Now, I know what I missed and am pleased and nourished by the sight of old Black people. Ageing for me is like completing a circle."

Southwark Council's **Black and Minority Ethnic Workers' Consultative Group** was launched on October 13, 2004. Supported by management and all of the trade unions, the group aims to create a better understanding of staff's views about employment issues and how the council delivers services to meet the needs of the Black and minority ethnic community. At the launch, Anthony Berry, principal project

Southwark Police Commendation Awards, HMS Belfast, June 29, 2004 (from left to right) David Meaghur, Cecile Lothian (Mayor of Southwark, 1993-94), Borough Commander Ian Thomas, Cllr Anne Yates (Mayor of Southwark), Althea Smith, Stephen Bourne, Maureen Lynch and Inspector Bradley Walter (Metropolitan Police Service)

officer, said: "The group will be about partnership rather than an adversarial role. The key to its success is to get people from across the council involved – to work with management to develop improvements that BME staff recognise."

Cllr. Columba Blango was born in Sierra Leone and took part in the first West African Games in 1977. At the 1980 Olympic Games in Moscow he took part in the Decathlon. In 1998 he was elected as the Liberal Democrat councillor for Dockyard Ward in Southwark, and served as the Mayor of Southwark from 2003-04. Columba is the executive member for Culture in the London Borough of Southwark.

Carl Campbell Dance Company 7 celebrated its 25th anniversary in 2004 with events for Southwark's Black History Month. Based in Peckham, its founder, Carl Campbell, was born in Jamaica and moved to Britain in the 1960s. Carl says, "When I started performing I never wanted to form a Company, spiritually that decision was made for me and twenty-five years later I realise that it was the right decision. I wanted to be a mechanic, but now I know that there was no other way that I could help build bridges between people, to change attitudes and perceptions that increase tolerance and understanding from people of different ages, or cultures. If I could have done that professionally I would still be in the West End, but working with schools and communities you are able to really make a difference. CCDC7 is dedicated to demystifying this myth and demonstrating to people, particularly young Black people that we must be proud of Black arts organisations, especially those that have existed for a long time. That is what twenty-five years of the Company means to me."

The **Cuming Museum** in Walworth Road SE17 is home to the rich and unusual collection of the Cuming family and the museum of Southwark's history. Today's remit is to collect material that relates to Southwark and represents all of Southwark's communities. The Museum has made a deliberate effort to address cultural diversity and holds a special place in the Southwark community. In recent years some untold stories have been presented through an incredibly diverse programme of exhibitions and workshops. For example, the superb *Lost and Found* exhibition (see chapter 1) that explored the early presence of Black African, Caribbean and Asian people in Southwark, *Home from Home* (Latin American elders), the history of Millwall Football Club, and *Untold Origins*, which told the story of migrations of people and cultures over thousands of years from Guyana to the Caribbean and then onto Southwark. These have all succeeded in drawing a wide, diverse audience unlike other museums that attract mostly white, well-educated, middle-class audiences.

Cllr. Dora Dixon Fyle was born in Sierra Leone and, in 1998, she became the first African-born woman to be elected as a Councillor in Southwark. Since that time she has served as a Labour Councillor for Camberwell Ward. Also an actress, Dora has appeared in a number of television dramas including *EastEnders* and *Great Moments in Aviation*.

Chiwetel Ejiofor started acting at the age of thirteen at Dulwich College and just eight years later appeared as the West African interpreter in Steven Spielberg's film *Amistad* (1997). Born in Forest Gate, east London, he moved to West Norwood with his Nigerian parents, and was educated at Dulwich College in Southwark. Following several seasons with the

National Youth Theatre, Chiwetel was critically acclaimed for his stage role in the National Theatre's production of *Blue/Orange* (2000). For his memorable performance, the young actor was named Outstanding Newcomer by the London Evening Standard's Theatre Awards, and was nominated for a Laurence Olivier Theatre Award. In 2002, Chiwetel received further acclaim – and another award from the London Evening Standard – for his portrayal of Okwe, a doctor forced to work in secrecy because he is an illegal immigrant, in the film *Dirty Pretty Things*. He has recently pursued his film career in America, appearing in Woody Allen's *Melinda and Melinda* (2004) and Spike Lee's *She Hate Me* (2004).

Tayo Fatunla is a cartoonist whose book *Our Roots – Black History Sketchbook* was reissued with great success in 2004. Over 100 illustrations of Black historical figures and events are featured in *Our Roots*, including several mentioned in *Speak of Me As I Am:* Windrush Arrivants, Norman Beaton, Mary Seacole, Damilola Taylor and Bert Williams. First serialised in *The Voice* newspaper, they were then syndicated in more than 30 newspapers. Tayo is employed by Southwark Libraries.

From Boyhood to Manhood Foundation was set up in Peckham in 1996 by Decima Francis and Uanu Seshmi in response to parental concern about the number of young Black boys being excluded from school. Says Uanu Seshmi, "Young people start our programme filled with an anger and confusion they can't explain. They feel their community blames them for every crime and it's easy for them to be hostile back. Acting bad gives them an identity. It attracts the attention they want and gets people's recognition. We help them find a self-esteem that doesn't need to be proved every night on the streets."

Cllr. Aubyn Graham was born in Jamaica and has been a community development worker in Southwark for many years. A long-standing Labour councillor, Aubyn was elected to serve the Lyndhurst Ward in 1982, a position he held until 1998 when he changed to the Lane Ward. Aubyn served as the Mayor of Southwark from 1995-96.

Reg Gyasi has been active in community affairs since coming to live in
Southwark in 1981. He has also been involved with the local council and
policing, as well as Tenants' Associations.

Muriel Hunte is an actress whose career spans five decades and some
notable film and television productions. These include Ken Loach's
ground-breaking BBC drama-documentary *Cathy Come Home* (1966),
the popular comedy film *The Full Monty* (1997), Lennie James's award-
winning television drama *Storm Damage* (1999) starring Adrian Lester,
and, more recently, the hit BBC comedy *Little Britain* (2004). Muriel has
received a Civic Award from the London Borough of Southwark for her
community work.

Sunny Lambe is a management consultant who has worked for many
years in the community/voluntary sector. He has assisted in building
a support framework for Black Minority Ethnic communities in London,
and particularly in Southwark. Sunny is currently the Chair of the
Southwark Black Heritage Organisation (SBHO).

Cecile Lothian (see photo on page 88) was the Mayor of Southwark in
1993-94 and a former member of the Metropolitan Police Authority.

S. I. Martin lives in Camberwell where he works as a researcher and
writer of Black history. He has worked as a journalist for *The Voice* and
Bulletin. He is the author of two books: a novel, *Incomparable World*
(1996), which tells the story of three Black exiles living in eighteenth-
century London, and a non-fiction title, *Britain's Slave Trade* (1999),
published to accompany a television series screened on Channel 4.

Sir Herman Ouseley was born in Guyana and came to Britain when
he was eleven. He lived in Peckham for 44 years and has had a
distinguished career in local government. His many appointments
include Head of the Greater London Council's Ethnic Minorities Unit;
Chief Executive of the Inner London Education Authority (the first Black
person to hold such an office); Chief Executive of the London Borough
of Lambeth; and, from 1993-2000, Chair of the Commission for Racial

Equality. Knighted in 1997, four years later he was raised to the peerage as Baron Ouseley of Peckham Rye. Herman is known as someone with a track record of changing organisations, getting results and championing the cause of equality and fair treatment for all.

Althea Smith (see photo on page 88) is a political campaigner and committed community volunteer who has chaired the Southwark Police and Community Consultative Group for many years. Althea moved to London from Jamaica when she was thirteen and settled in Peckham in 1978. For her work as an adviser to the murder investigation of Peckham schoolboy Damilola Taylor, Althea received a Metropolitan Police Volunteer Award in 2002. She says, "I love Peckham...Peckham can be improved [but] you need to have a community behind changes, so behind the police, behind the politicians, you need to have a community."

The **Southwark Race and Equalities Council** offers advice relating to race issues for minority ethnic communities and the general public. It also runs youth offenders schemes and a racial incidents forum.

The **Southwark Young People's Magazine Project** (formerly the *Peckham Young People's Magazine Project*) caters for young people in the borough aged between fourteen and twenty-one years. The Project aims to develop young people's skills in journalism, graphic design and photography. The Project also publishes a free monthly magazine with a circulation of 10,000. In 2001 the Project received The Philip Lawrence Award, administered by the National Youth Agency for outstanding achievement in active citizenship by young people. One of the Project's many initiatives is the short film *The Blox*. Written and directed by Damien Bent, it was filmed by members of the Project in and around Peckham in October 2002. *The Blox* tells the story of two brothers in a tale of drugs, revenge and misplaced loyalty, and immediately grabbed the attention of young people and adults when it was shown at the Peckham Multiplex cinema.

Su-Elise, a member of popular rhythm and blues trio Mis-Teeq, spent most of her teenage years in Southwark, growing up in Surrey Quays and West

Cover of Peckham Young People's Magazine Project (2002)

Dulwich. As soon as she could walk, she took ballet and tap classes, and started drama and singing lessons at the age of seven. She met fellow band members Alesha and Sabrina while she was auditioning for another group. Their first single, *Why*, stormed the charts in 2001. This was followed by a string of top ten hits, two critically acclaimed albums, and numerous awards and nominations. Although their origins are in the British garage scene, Mis-Teeq's crossover appeal means they're as much at home playing Glastonbury as the Queen's Jubilee concert at Buckingham Palace. Mis-Teeq's smash hit single *Scandalous* was featured in the Halle Berry film *Catwoman*. In 2004 Su-Elise told *Southwark Life*: "I've moved out to Kent now but my parents still live in Dulwich, so I come back all the time. It's my home. I feel most comfortable here out of everywhere."

Pat Tulloch is the founding Director of Southwark Action for Voluntary Organisations (SAVO), the borough co-ordinating body for the voluntary and community sector in Southwark. This is made up of 1,600 organisations and groups, 18,000 individuals, and worth around £655m to the economy of this borough. Pat is a community activist with twenty-five years experience of working in the voluntary and community sector. She says: "The thing that motivates me most is the sense of injustice that exists in most minority communities, and the meaningless loss of lives, whether that is physical or psychological. When a Black woman has a male child she does not dream of whether he will attend University, her dream is whether he will live beyond the age of twenty-five."

Debbie Welch died before this book was commissioned but I want to include her because she was a friend whose outstanding work in the Southwark community should not be forgotten. Debbie started work as a youth and community worker in Peckham in the 1960s. She joined Southwark Council in 1986 and as a Labour councillor she represented the former Liddle Ward, between Camberwell and Peckham. She was outspoken on issues such as social care and health. As Deputy Leader of Southwark Council in the early 1990s, Cllr. Welch was one of the very few Black women to reach such a senior position in a London local authority. In later years, she was recognised for campaigning on youth crime, and for her work as an adviser to the murder investigation of Peckham schoolboy Damilola Taylor, for which she received a Metropolitan Police Volunteer Award in 2002. Says Cllr Aubyn Graham, "Debbie contributed significantly to the community and quality of life for people in Southwark." Debbie passed away in January 2004. In 2001, Debbie's son, Dominic, gave a speech at the opening of the Damilola Taylor Centre in Peckham.

Southwark Culture and Heritage Services/ Southwark Libraries

This book has been commissioned by the Culture and Heritage Services Section of Southwark Council. Culture and Heritage Services provides the Cuming Museum, Livesey Museum for Children, Kingswood House and Southwark Local History Library. It aims to engage local people with their heritage and history and offers unique and inspiring opportunities for people to come together to learn about each other's lives and cultures: "We believe our service is the most significant local cultural resource in Southwark. It inspires pride in our diverse culture and history and challenges traditional perceptions and entrenched stereotypes." Part of the core purpose of Southwark's Culture and Heritage Services is to engage with and promote diversity in Southwark and work with the local community to tell the untold stories of the contribution that Black and minority ethnic communities have made to the history and development of Southwark.

Further information about some of the people featured in *Speak of Me As I Am* can be found in Southwark Libraries, including the award-winning Peckham Library (Peckham High Street) and smaller community libraries in the borough. The Local History Library is located at 211 Borough High Street SE1.

Southwark Libraries aim to provide a welcoming and stimulating environment for all library users. Their many services include free book lending and reference services. Each library has a Black writing section covering both fiction and non-fiction.

Access to the catalogue and further information about Southwark Libraries can be found on Southwark's website (www.southwark.gov.uk). The online catalogue allows you to search for and reserve any title available in Southwark.

At the time of writing, the books listed below are currently available.

Other titles by Stephen Bourne
Aunt Esther's Story (1991) with Esther Bruce
A Ship and a Prayer (1999) with Sav Kyriacou
Sophisticated Lady: A Celebration of Adelaide Hall (2001)
Black in the British Frame – The Black Experience in British Film and Television (2001)
Black and Asian Performance at the Theatre Museum: A User's Guide (2003) with Susan Croft and Dr. Alda Terracciano
Elisabeth Welch: Soft Lights and Sweet Music (2005)

General
Hakim Adi, *The History of the African and Caribbean Communities in Britain* (1995)
Patrick Augustus, *Babyfather* (1994)
John D. Beasley, *The Story of Peckham and Nunhead* (1999)
Mary Boast, *The Story of Camberwell* (1996)
David Bygott, *Black and British* (1992)
Paul Edwards and David Dabydeen, *Black Writers in Britain 1760-1890* (1991)
Tayo Fatunla, *Our Roots* (2004)
Nigel File and Chris Power, *Black Settlers in Britain 1555-1958* (1981)
Peter Fryer, *Staying Power – The History of Black People in Britain* (1984)
Peter Fryer, *Black People in the British Empire – An Introduction* (1989)
Jeffrey Green, *Black Edwardians – Black People in Britain 1901-1914* (1998)
Shirley Harrison and Sally Evemy, *Southwark: Who Was Who* (2001)
John Hughes (editor), *Who's Who of Black Achievers* (1999)
Courttia Newland and Kadija Sesay (editors), *IC3 – The Penguin Book of New Black Writing in Britain* (2000)
Susan Okokon, *Black Londoners 1880-1990* (1998)
Sukhdev Sandhu, *London Calling – How Black and Asian Writers Imagined a City* (2003)
Edward Scobie, *Black Britannia* (1972)
Marika Sherwood, *Many Struggles – West Indian Workers and Service Personnel in Britain* (1939-45) ((1985)

James Walvin, *Making the Black Atlantic – Britain and the African Diaspora* (2000)

**Camberwell's First Black Citizen and
Shakespeare's Othello at the Globe**
William Harnett Blanch, *The Parish of Camberwell* (1875)
Leslie Dunton-Downer and Alan Riding, *Essential Shakespeare Handbook* (2004)
Paul Edwards (editor), *Equiano's Travels* (1967)
S. I. Martin, *Britain's Slave Trade* (1999)
James Walvin, *Black Ivory – A History of British Slavery* (1992)

Mary Seacole
Harriet Castor, *Mary Seacole* (2001)
John Malam, *Mary Seacole* (1999)
Jane Robinson, *Mary Seacole: The Black Nightingale* (2005)
Mary Seacole, *The Wonderful Adventures of Mary Seacole in Many Lands* (1984)
Brian Williams, *The Life and World of Mary Seacole* (2003)

Dr. Harold Moody
David A. Vaughan, *Negro Victory* (1950)

Una Marson
Delia Jarrett-Macauley, *The Life of Una Marson 1905-65* (1998)

Paul Robeson
Martin Bauml Duberman, *Paul Robeson* (1989)
Scott Ehrlich, *Paul Robeson* (1989)
Jeffrey C. Stewart, *Paul Robeson: Artist and Citizen* (1998)

Sam King and
Empire Windrush
Floella Benjamin, *Coming to England* (1995)
The Black Cultural Archives, *The Windrush Legacy* (1998)
Vivienne Francis, *With Hope in Their Eyes* (1998)
Peter Fryer, *The Politics of Windrush* (1999)
Sam King, *Climbing Up the Rough Side of the Mountain* (1998)
Mike Phillips and Trevor Phillips, *Windrush – The Irresistible Rise of Multi-Racial Britain* (1998)

Tony Sewell, *Keep on Moving – The Windrush Legacy* (1998)

Marika Sherwood, *Claudia Jones – A Life in Exile* (1999)

Onyekachi Wambu (editor), *Empire Windrush – Fifty Years of Writing About Black Britain* (1999)

Norman Beaton

Norman Beaton (interview) in Jim Pines (editor), *Black and White in Colour – Black People in British Television Since 1936* (1992)

Rio Ferdinand and Chris Eubank

Wensley Clarkson, *Rio!* (2003)

Chris Eubank, *Chris Eubank – The Autobiography* (2003)

Cover of Sam King's autobiography

Oxford Dictionary of National Biography (Oxford University Press) Sixty volumes are available in Newington Reference Library, 155-157 Walworth Road SE17 and among the 50,000 biographies are the following Black historical figures who are mentioned in *Speak of Me As I Am*. The name of the author follows:

Amanda Ira Aldridge (Stephen Bourne), **Ira Aldridge** (Heidi J. Holder), **Norman Beaton** (Stephen Bourne), **George Polgreen Bridgetower** (W. B. Squire, revised by David J. Golby), **Esther Bruce** (Stephen Bourne), **William Cuffay** (Peter Fryer), **Belle Davis** (Jeffrey Green and Rainer E. Lotz), **Olaudah Equiano** (James Walvin), **Len Johnson** (Gary Shaw), **Claudia Jones** (Marika Sherwood), **Una Marson** (Denise de Caires Narain), **Dr. Harold Moody** (David Killingray), **Paul Robeson** (Hakim Adi), **Ignatius Sancho** (Vincent Carretta), **Mary Seacole** (Alan Palmer).

About the author

Born in St. Giles's Hospital, Camberwell, and raised on a council estate in Peckham, Stephen Bourne is one of Britain's leading authorities on Black history. He is a member of the Black and Asian Studies Association, a regular contributor to *Black Filmmaker* magazine, and has presented Black History Month events in Southwark for many years. He is the author of several Black history books including *Aunt Esther's Story, A Ship and a Prayer, Sophisticated Lady – A Celebration of Adelaide Hall, Black in the British Frame – The Black Experience in British Film and Television* and *Elisabeth Welch: Soft Lights and Sweet Music.*

Stephen has organised many film and television events for the National Film Theatre including tributes to the film careers of such Black stars as Ethel Waters (1993), Elisabeth Welch (1994), Paul Robeson (1998) and Edric Connor (1998). In 1988 he graduated from the London College of Printing at the Elephant and Castle with a Bachelor of Arts Degree in Film and Television. For television he has been a researcher on Channel 4's *Sophisticated Lady* (1989, a profile of Adelaide Hall), Channel 4's *We Sing and We Dance* (1992, a profile of the Nicholas Brothers), and BBC-2's *Black and White in Colour* (1992, a two-part history of Black people in British television). For the BBC's *Windrush* season in 1998, he researched and scripted Radio 2's *Their Long Voyage Home*, presented by Sir Trevor McDonald. Stephen has been interviewed in several documentaries including Channel 4's *Black Divas* (1996), BBC-2's *Paul Robeson: Speak of Me As I Am* (1998), *Paul Robeson: Here I Stand* (1999, an American Masters presentation) and BBC Radio 3's *Stage and Screen.*

Stephen has received two Race in the Media awards from the Commission for Racial Equality. For *Black in the British Frame* he was shortlisted for *The Voice* newspaper's Black Community Award for Literature and received a Civic Award from the London Borough of Southwark.

In 1995 Stephen was instrumental in setting up the Southwark Anti-Homophobic Forum. As a result of the bridge-building work he had already accomplished with Southwark Police, in 1999 Stephen was asked to become a member of Southwark's Critical Incident Panel which he readily accepted. He has discharged this responsibility with enthusiasm and conscientiousness in a number of high-profile cases, most notably the murder of Peckham schoolboy Damilola Taylor.

In 2003, for his work as a community adviser to the police, he received a Metropolitan Police Volunteer Award from Commissioner Sir John Stevens and Mayor Ken Livingstone at a ceremony in City Hall in Southwark.

Index

Names

Aduaka, Newton I.   10, 18, 74-75
Agard, Sandra   86
Akindayini, Segun   86
Aldridge, Amanda Ira   55
Aldridge, Ira   8-9, 14, 25-28, 55
Augustus, Patrick   86

Barber, Paul   72
Beaton, Norman   17, 73-74, 90
Beethoven   24
Bellos, Linda   52, 87
Berry, Anthony   87
Blanch, William Harnett   19
Blango, Columba   17, 62, 88
Blanke, John   12
Boast, Mary   19, 41
Bogle, Paul   63
Bonnick, Keith   22
Bridgetower,
    George Polgreen   15, 24
Brooke, Alex   iv, 1-2
Bruce, Esther   6-9, 60-61
Bruce, Joseph   7

Campbell, Carl   88
Carl Campbell
    Dance Company 7   88
Clarke, Dr. Cecil Belfield   16, 48
Coleridge-Taylor, Samuel   7
Connor, Edric   68, 99
Cuffay, William   24

Davis, Belle   15, 39, 41
Dixon Fyle, Dora   89
Duffy, David Anthony   14, 24

Ejiofor, Chiwetel   89-90
Ekpenyon, Oku   27

Elizabeth I   12-13, 20-21
Equiano, Olaudah   3, 14
Eubank, Chris   83-84

Fatunla, Tayo   90
Ferdinand, Rio   3, 9, 17-18,
    81-82, 84-85
Fisk Jubilee Singers   15, 31-35
Francis, Decima   90
Fryer, Peter   8, 31

Garvey, Marcus   7, 56, 86
Graham, Aubyn   17, 52, 69, 90, 94
Green, Jeffrey   36
Gyasi, Reg   91

Hall, Adelaide   60, 99
Henriques, Julian   74
Henriques, Pauline   42, 45
Henry, Lenny   79
Hill, Errol   29
Hogarth, William   13
Honeyghan, Lloyd   82
Hunte, Muriel   91

James, C. L. R.   49, 81
Jean-Baptiste, Marianne   9, 17-18,
    76-80
Johnson, Jack   7
Johnson, Juber   22
Johnson, Len   16, 81-82
Jones, Claudia   17, 66-68

Kenyatta, Jomo   49, 55, 81
King, Dr. Martin Luther   10, 68
King, Sam   3, 9-11, 16-17, 62-70

Laine, Cleo   58, 60
Lambe, Sunny   91
Lawrence, Doreen   76, 79

Lawrence, Stephen	79	Porter, Maggie	32
Livingstone, Mayor Ken	100	Powell, Enoch	6
L'Ouverture, Toussaint	63	Primero, John	13, 20-22
Lothian, Cecile	17, 88, 91	Profitt, Russell	52
Lotz, Rainer E.	41	Prophett, Benjamin	14, 24
McDonald, Gary	71	Reckord, Barry	45
McDonald, Sir Trevor	99	Roberts, Benjamin George	22
Mandela, Nelson	10	Roberts, Norwell	66
Mark, Connie	31	Robeson, Eslanda	55
Marson, Una	16, 48-49	Robeson, Paul	9, 16, 39, 44, 49,
Martin, S. I.	72, 91		53-58, 60, 81, 99
Massive, Mikey	80	Robeson Jr, Paul	55
Moody, Charles	16, 47, 49-50		
Moody, Christine	47, 50	Sancho, Ignatius	14
Moody, Garth	47, 50	Scobie, Edward	8
Moody, Harold	47, 50	Seacole, Mary	3, 8-9, 14,
Moody, Dr. Harold	9-11, 15-18,		29-31, 90
	46-52	Seshmi, Uanu	90
Moody, Joan	47	Severus, Septimius	12
Moody, Ronald	47, 50	Sewell, Tony	62
Morgan, Luce	13, 21	Shakespeare, William	9, 13,
Mosley, Oswald	67		21, 28-29
Munroe, Carmen	73-74	Sherwood, Marika	62
		Shyllon, Folarin	8
Neville, Joyce	56	Smith, Althea	88, 92
Newell, Russell	74	Smith, Augustus	42-43
Nightingale, Florence	31	Smith, Connie	15, 42-45
Nkrumah, Kwame	49	Smith, Morgan	15, 28-29
		Spurgeon, Charles Haddon	33
O'Connell, Rory	62	Stanford, Gold Teeth	67
Otway, Tim	19, 35, 44, 51	Stevens, Sir John	100
Ouseley, Sir Herman	91-92	Stowe, Harriet Beecher	15
		Su-Elise	92-93
Padmore, George	81		
Parks, Rosa	10	Taylor, Damilola	iv, 1-2, 85, 87,
Parsons, Mark	1-2		90, 92, 94, 100
Phillips, Mike	62	Taylor, Robert	iv, 1-2
Phillips, Sir Trevor	3-4, 62	Tulloch, Pat	93-94
Poitier, Sidney	71		

Victoria, Queen   14-15, 24,
                           30, 32-33

Walker, George   36-37
Walvin, James   8
Washington, Denzel   71-72
Welch, Debbie   94
Welch, Elisabeth   7, 9, 16, 45, 55,
                           58-61, 99
Williams, Bert   36-39, 90
Williams, Elizabeth   22
Wilmer, Val   7
Woollacott, Ron   46
Worrell, Trix   72-73

Younge, Gary   78

Places

Albany Road   67
Archbishop Michael Ramsey
Technology College   8

Bellenden Junior School   83
Bellenden Road   73
Bermondsey   22, 82
Bishopsmead   66
Blackfriars Road   14-16, 25, 81
Blucher Road   66
Brandon Estate   82
Borough High Street   4, 95
Brook Drive   45
Brunswick Square   48
Burgess Park   18, 52
Butterfly Walk   52

Camberwell   8, 14, 17, 20-22,
                24, 65, 67, 76, 83, 91
Camberwell Church Street   21

Camberwell Church
   Street Library   8
Camberwell College of Arts   1
Camberwell Gate   15, 34
Camberwell Green   17
Camberwell Green
   Congregational Church   17, 52
Camberwell Palace
   of Varieties   3, 15-16, 40-41,
                           43, 61
Camberwell Police Station   52
Camberwell Road   17, 65-66
Camelot Primary School   84
Chumleigh Gardens   18, 52
Crown Theatre   15, 36, 38
Cuming Museum   21, 89, 95

Damilola Taylor Centre   94
Dr. Harold Moody Park   10, 52
Dulwich   93
Dulwich College   89

Elephant and Castle   9, 15-16, 33,
                48, 53, 56-57, 83, 99
Elephant and Castle
   Shopping Centre   86
Emmanuel Church   17, 66

Friary Estate   84

Gaumont Palace Cinema   38
Globe Theatre, Bankside   13, 21

Imperial War Museum   11

King's Grove   15, 47
King's Road   15-16, 47
Kingswood House   95

Leyton Gardens   84

Leyton Square 18
Livesey Museum for Children 95
London College of Printing 9, 99

Metropolitan Tabernacle 15, 33-35

Newington 23
Newington Causeway 16, 48
New Kent Road 77
North Peckham Estate 1, 72
North Peckham Library 77, 84
Nunhead 83
Nunhead Library 10-11

Obelisk, The 25
Old Kent Road 77
Oliver Goldsmith
Primary School 1, 5

Peckham 1-3, 5-10, 15-18,
24, 36, 46, 48, 65,
67-68, 71-75, 77, 81,
83-85, 90-92, 94, 99-100
Peckham Bookplace 8-9
Peckham High Street 15, 36,
38, 95
Peckham Hill Street Library 8
Peckham Hippodrome
Picture Palace 38
Peckham Leisure Centre 84
Peckham Library 11, 86, 95
Peckham Manor
Secondary School 83
Peckham Police Station 38
Peckham Road 1, 5-6, 68
Peckham Rye Park 84
Peckham Settlement 84

Queen's Road 16-17, 48, 52

Ring, The 16, 81
Rotherhithe 22-23
Royal Surrey Gardens 14, 30
Rye Lane 8

St. George's Circus 25
St. George's Roman
Catholic Cathedral 45
St. Giles's Church,
Camberwell 13, 19-20
St. Giles's Hospital,
Camberwell 17, 77, 99
St. Michael and
All Angels' School 8
St. Saviour's and
St. Olave's School 77
Sears Street 17, 65
Sojourner Truth Centre 11
Southampton Way 1
South London Palace 15
Southwark Cathedral 62, 70
Southwark Local
History Library 33, 95
Surrey Quays 92
Surrey Theatre 14-15, 25-26,
28-29

Thomas Carlton
Secondary School 83
Trocadero Cinema 16, 53, 56-57

Walworth 30
Walworth Road 14, 21, 34, 83, 89
Wren Road 17, 52
Wyndham Road 14, 24